BROTHER SHAD'S DANDELIONS

A NURSING HOME RESIDENT STRUGGLES WITH RETIREMENT ISSUES

CHARLES T. CLAUSER

2017

Copyrighted © 2017 Charles T. Clauser
All rights reserved.

This book is a work of historical fiction. Names, characters, businesses, organizations, places, events, and incidents either are a product of the author's imagination or are used fictitiously. Any resemblance to actual persons, living or dead, events or locals is unintentional and entirely coincidental.

No part of this publication may be reproduced, stored in a retrieval system, or transmitted in any form or by any means -- electronic, mechanical, photocopy, recording, or any other -- except for brief quotations in printed reviews, without the prior permission of the publisher.

Published by Dad Guiseppi Publishing, 3316 N. Heritage Avenue, Springfield, MO 65803.

Unless otherwise indicated, Scripture references are taken from the New King James Version (NKJV). Copyright © 1982 by Thomas Nelson, Inc. Used by permission. All rights reserved.

Verses quoted from the King James Version (KJV) are taken from The Holy Bible. Copyright © 1970, by Thomas Nelson, Inc. Used by permission. All rights reserved.

Italics used in quotations from Scripture at the beginning of each chapter have been inserted by the author for added emphasis.

Printed by CreateSpace, an Amazon Company
Printed in the United States of America
ISBN-10: 0-692-93458-8
ISBN-13: 978-0-692-93458-6

TABLE OF CONTENTS

CONTENTS - iii
REVIEWS FROM READERS - v
PREFACE - ix
FOREWORD - xiii

PART ONE
SPRING—CHANGES FROM A FORMER HOME - 15
1. SHADOWS OF FORMER CONQUESTS - 17
2. SUDDEN ACCIDENTS SURMOUNTED - 31
3. SUPPRESSED ANGER EXPLODES - 45

PART TWO
SUMMER—CHANGES TO A NEW LIFE-STYLE - 59
4. STEWARDSHIP SETTLES AGE DIFFERENCES - 61
5. SUCCESSFUL BIBLE BITS - 75
6. SUMMER DEATH UNEXPECTED - 97

PART THREE
AUTUMN—CHANGES IN PERSEVERANCE - 115
7. SECURITY QUESTIONED ABOUT FINANCES - 117
8. SPACE SHARED WITH OTHERS - 133
9. STRONG MEMORIES OF YESTERYEAR - 153

PART FOUR
WINTER—CHANGES THROUGH CRISES EVENTS - 171
10. SENILITY INTRUDES UNINVITED - 173
11. SPECIAL VISITORS MINISTER - 191
12. SALVATION SETTLES DESTINY - 209

EPILOGUE—FIVE YEARS LATER - 231
END NOTES - 233
AUTHOR'S BIOGRAPHY - 235

REVIEWS FROM READERS

James D. Wilkins
Former Nebraska District Superintendent, Assemblies of God
President of Assist Ministries, Inc.
Springfield, Missouri

"Through a variety of dialogues, this book will take you into the bantering conversations of Brother Shad and his aging caregiver. It is a human interest story that provides a sometimes humorous and sometimes painful peek into the life of a dear elderly man who knows his memory is slipping away. If you are looking for a story of high drama and intrigue, this is not it. If you are looking for a sensitive glimpse into issues and challenges you or a loved one may face in the future or if you want to vicariously enjoy the encouragement a caregiver can give, then read on."

Chaplain Darryl Paddock
Maranatha Village
Springfield, Missouri

"Through a series of brief vignettes, this author has managed to highlight several critical issues that confront many of our elderly people today. Although Brother Shad is a fictional character, his experiences of aging and transitioning into a nursing home setting are very real. With all of the accompanying physical and mental issues there is the added stress of moving into an environment where independence and privacy are almost nonexistent. Also demonstrated in this story is the tremendous impact that supportive family and friends, as well as personal faith, can play in the life of an elderly person struggling to cope with the emotions and feelings that accompany this kind of change."

Dave Weston, National Director
Senior Adult Ministries
Assemblies of God

"In *Brother Shad's Dandelions*, Charles Clauser permits the reader an inside view into the lives of two people who are on the opposite side of a very real issue. Brother Shad, whose memory has rapidly deteriorated, is forced into a care facility. Aunt Matti, a close friend for many years, is committed to being a care-giver to the old gentleman, and is extremely attentive to his many needs. Although both characters are fictional, the complexities that each one faces in navigating the course of day-to-day life are real. Clauser's book offers insight into the 'world' of Brother Shad, along with its many challenges, and validates the significant and important role of the care-giver."

David W. Flower
Former A/G District Superintendent
Southern New England District

"*Brother Shad's Dandelions* is the fictional narrative of a kindly retired minister based on real life scenes. The venue is a retirement center. The story tells of the adjustments he makes with the help of loving family and close friends. It is a tender account of his faithful service to the other residents. There are many tugs on the heartstrings, such as when a dining room tablemate dies and he himself comes to the gates of heaven. It is an insightful and interesting read."

Dr. Jim W. Davis
Former Vice President of Research
Asia Pacific Theological Seminary
Baguio City, Luzon, Philippines

"The author, Charles Clauser, has been able to inspire his readers with the vibrant caring life style and friendship that can exist between elderly friends like Brother Shad and Aunt Matti as lived within a retirement community. The life style of caring for one another and contributing to their needs is contained within the daily intimate conversations and actions of loving and encouraging one another in the declining years of life. Bravo Mr. Clauser for the portrayal of life as God intended it to be during our declining years here on earth!"

Rev. Fred Chilton
Retired Assemblies of God Pastor,
National Christian Education Leader,
World Missions Staff Personnel.

"The fictional characters of Brother Shad and Aunt Matti in Charles Clauser's book, *Brother Shad's Dandelions,* give a true inside-out look at some of the difficulties along with the joys of retirement while living in a retirement center. The stories and settings depict the true realities of senior retirement and the ability to apply our faith along with other coping methods to make this time meaningful rather than despairing. The book with it's true to life scenes of the aging population would be great reading for those in retirement, those who are planning for future retirement, and the families of both."

David L. Nelson
Former South Dakota A/G District Superintendent

"Within the pages of this book you will meet very special people, each relating to a godly patriarch nearing the time of his earthly dismissal to heaven. Written through the lens of four life 'seasons,' you grasp a new perspective on the declining years of life. There's enough Gospel in this story to clearly reveal the way of salvation to any reader. Two realities of life, joy and sorrow, are intertwined in this heart-touching narrative. As you begin to read, the tender love of a true 'care giver' is revealed. When you finish you will truly desire to be more like Jesus, the ultimate 'care giver.'"

Robert Crabtree
Former Ohio District Superintendent
A/G European Missionary

"The descriptive word pictures painted by Charles Clauser portray the types of situations seniors living in a Christian retirement home may experience. The story line realistically serves as a guide to those approaching or in their senior years. The special friendship between *Brother Shad* and *Matti* demonstrates how two individuals, who have lost their marital partners, help one another as a brother and sister. I appreciated the author's use of Scripture throughout the book."

Kyle Dana, AG Financial Solutions
Senior Vice President Retirement Planning

"*Brother Shad's Dandelions* takes us on a reflective journey of an elderly man coming to the end of his life. Author Clauser captures the complexities of aging in today's care-home setting, both spiritually as well as relationally. The character of Brother Shad reminds us of the greater purpose we have in Christ and the impact that our lives have on those around us while his care-giver, Aunt Matti, demonstrates selflessness and servant hood. This book will bring encouragement to readers supporting elderly loved ones."

Dr. Roscoe Leach, retired pastor
Director, Pastoral Counseling, Christian Life Center
Bensalem, Pennsylvania

"Author Clauser has caught the delicate and fascinating interaction between two friends in their twilight years. Set in a care facility, Clauser explores the often perplexing events surrounding two wonderful people. *Brother Shad's Dandelions* presents a good read for anyone facing the deteriorating health of a loved one."

PREFACE

THIS FICTIONAL CHRISTIAN biography revolves around the life of a 94-year-old retired pastor, Brother Shad (Shadrach) Milburn, who hates dandelions and agonizes why God delays to take him "home." He releases his pent up frustration by engaging in daily walks around the outside of the City Center Retirement Home. Each excursion displays his determined efforts to pull up and destroy every dandelion within sight.

The aged minister suffers from dementia, minimal family visits, headaches, minor strokes, and loss of appetite. These infirmities halted his international pulpit ministry and disrupted his ministry in the Center. He struggles with feelings of despondency, misplaced anger and dependence on others for the fulfillment of his personal needs.

An 82-year-old, longtime ministerial friend, Aunt Matti (Matilda) Henderson, loves him like a brother. Through her compassionate concern, she becomes the major family caregiver for this aging minister. Personal assistance not supplied by the capable retirement staff causes her to drive in each day from her suburban home in order to provide extra attention and companionship for him.

Aunt Matti worked with Brother Shad for a short time in a mid-Western state 54 years earlier. Throughout her early years as a South Dakota farm girl, she learned to milk cows and played piano at district camp and council meetings. In later years, she ministered as a pastor's wife, and taught Sunday school classes. Thus, a life-long association developed between their families.

In the intervening years, she learned long-term care techniques by tending to her own elderly parents and other aging friends. Now, she realizes Brother Shad's physical condition may proceed toward deteriorated mental alertness and physical capabilities. She readily acknowledges, the Lord Jesus gave her strength to cope with each care-giving challenge.

Brother Shad's Dandelions portrays a nursing home resident who views life from the "inside-looking-out" at the world posture as opposed to a prospective resident who seeks answers for his questions posed from the "outside-looking-in" viewpoint.

The lives of two real-life senior citizens who struggled each day with their own retirement challenges provided the inspiration for this story. Actual events and episodes in the lives of these two persons provided the background for this fictional commentary.

The life stories of both protagonists would comprise volumes, since each experienced soul-wrenching heartache as well as blissful contentment in their own life journey. These two giants of Christian faith possessed an unusual caregiver-care receiver relationship at the time when these episodes were conceived. Events included in *Brother Shad's Dandelions* fictionalize the youth of both individuals, their latter-years' relationship in the retirement home culture, and certain other incidents of their extraordinary lives.

Activities and events in *Brother Shad's Dandelions* occur over a nine month period in the year 2007. Within each chapter, certain stated days of the week and hours of the day add perspective and continuity. Beneath each chapter title, a short scripture reference states a word of encouragement for family members who may seek adjustment for a type of problem described in a particular chapter. Throughout the text, subtitles describe particular dilemmas, situations, and predicaments encountered by the old man.

The four sections labeled spring, summer, fall, or winter, remind the reader of the progression of life stated by King Solomon in Ecclesiastes 3:1: "To everything there is a season, a time for every purpose under heaven."

A person 50 years of age or more, who faces either planned or forced retirement should seek answers to these questions: How will the onset of retirement affect my life? What preparations will I need to consider in order to face the challenges and responsibilities of life in my 70's, 80's, 90's, and perhaps beyond?

Will my family provide care for me in my latter years? Will they extend follow-up support for me? Will a move into a retirement complex become a necessity for me? What quality of life might I expect in a retirement home? What situation in my life might require a transfer into an assisted-living facility?

How long might I live independent of assisted care? What might I expect with a move into an independent-living or an assisted-living facility? How might I keep active and productive once I become a resident in a retirement complex? How might I prepare myself to cope with living in a retirement home?

Various factors might influence a person's move into a retirement complex or into an assisted-living environment. This kind of life-style change may develop in a variety of ways for any new resident.[1]

Persons who might consider the move of a relative or friend into a retirement facility, need not leave the total responsibility for care of their loved one with the staff. Instead, family members should devise a plan when possible, to include younger relatives as part of the transition process for an older family member or friend.

The gathering together of total family participation establishes a welcome factor in resettlement for a person who retires from active ministry, secular work, or transfers in from a home-care situation. This resultant reduction in stress helps build additional family memories and promotes a comfortable home-away-from home experience. The new resident needs continual family care, involvement, and expressions of *agape* (Christ-like) and *phileo* (brotherly) love. Resettlement efforts by both the family and retirement staff help relieve frustration which might otherwise tend to overwhelm the new occupant.

The trauma of a move into an assisted-living accommodation can be reduced for a senior person if both family and resident know ahead of time of pending changes in his or her life style. *Brother Shad's Dandelions* identifies several areas of these senior adult moments.

Throughout my missionary service, I found myself in a venue of interchange with young people—25-, 35-, 45-, and 55-year-old members of a society. Settled now in independent living at a retirement center, I find myself interacting with 65-, 75-, 85-, and 95-year-old retirees who cope with different stages of activity, emotional health, and physical fitness. Ministry in this type of facility sets no time constraints, because each of our neighbors and other senior residents evidence their own particular needs.

The technical assistance of Ann M. Floyd, Stanley L. Morlin, Richard L. Schoonover, Diane Awbrey, Jim Cole-Rous, Rob Sorbo, and Michael James Williams provided valuable insights for me in the preparation of this book.

I wish to express sincere gratitude to my helpmate and wife, Mary, for extended periods of time I set aside to prepare this manuscript. Her constant caregiving for me continues into its sixth decade. God blessed me with a precious woman as my life partner. Thank you, Dear! CTC.

FOREWORD

CHARLES CLAUSER DREW from his personal relationship with two wonderful individuals, who left an indelible imprint on hundreds of lives. This inspirational story will touch your life and draw you into the trials and triumphs of these precious saints. Rooted in scripture, each chapter provides keen insight into the challenges and opportunities that come with old age and life in a retirement center.

I served as an administrator of a retirement center for 13 years which allowed me to witness how families react when faced with the decision of what to do when a loved one no longer copes with the physical or mental capacity to live on their own.

A move into a care facility not only requires the resident to make adjustments, but causes family and friends to reorder their lives. Information shared on these pages can serve as a pattern for continued fruitfulness in the latter years of life.

Brother Shad's Dandelions will speak in different ways to individuals. Some will see themselves in the role of the old saint who experiences a change in residency and a loss of total independence. Others will relate to the compassionate caregiver who ministers and uplifts residents in difficult circumstances. If you are the child or grandchild of a parent or grandparent who resides in an assisted-living facility, may you feel inspired to maintain meaningful contact with your loved one, who will consider you a godsend and will bless your presence.

Evident in these pages, God purposes and plans good things for each person who lives in a retirement center regardless of age, previous vocation, or former place of residency. I trust this book will speak to persons who enjoy employment at a retirement center or nursing home, because each day your ministry there can make a difference in the lives of many individuals.

My prayer for you after you read this fictional story: receive encouragement to brighten your corner of God's creation.

Kenneth R. Tripp
A Retired Care-Giver

PART ONE

SPRING: CHANGES FROM A FORMER HOME

Our citizenship is in heaven.
Philippians 3:20

Therefore, if anyone is in Christ, he is a new creation; old things have passed away; behold, all things have become new.
2 Corinthians 3:1

CHAPTER ONE

SHADOWS OF FORMER CONQUESTS

I will not leave you nor forsake you.
Joshua 1:5

"MATTI, I NEED HELP"
MONDAY, MARCH 26, 7:00 A.M.

"MATTI," THE TELEPHONE CALL jolted her body before its regular wake-up time. The scratchy voice on the other end pleaded, "I need help. I can't find my glasses."

"Brother Shad," Aunt Matti tried to gather her senses. Her dry mouth, squeaked between attempts to clear her throat. "If (cough) you don't find your glasses by 10:00 a.m. (wheeze) when I come to see you, we will ask your duty nurse for assistance.

In the meantime, please finish your breakfast (cough). I know the attendant served you earlier. Drink your orange juice and eat your ham slice. You need to muster up strength for our jaunt to Drake's Market for cough drops and hair oil. Okay?"

"Yes, Matti. I thought I placed them on my night stand. I didn't knock them off and I can't find them in my shirt pocket. . . . I know I left my glasses here in this room."

Aunt Matti, a bit irritated by his bombastic voice, held the phone away from her ear. "Bye for now, Brother Shad." She threw aside the covers and dangled her feet over the edge of her bed, "I shall sign off and go prepare my breakfast. I feel hungry. And Brother Shad, please shave before I come this morning. We may see friends who might want to have lunch with us."

"Yes, Ma'am. Will do. See you later." After he hung up, he considered Matti's persistence. *I know of no one else who can help me like you, dear lady. Why do you neglect yourself just for me?*

"Lord," he mumbled as he looked around his bathroom again for the missing glasses, "I wouldn't know what to do without Matti's help. Please keep your hand upon her. You know I pray for her first thing each day. Please keep her safe from harm and any disaster, like a car accident. Her personal care and encouragement blesses several of us at the City Center.

"Aah, why did I place my specks on the back of the toilet bowl? Terrible place. They wouldn't flush well. Mister Shadrach Theodore Milburn, collect your wits, you idiot."

Matti lifted a prayer to the Lord, then scurried around her kitchen, and prepared a cup of coffee. Watching the coffee pot percolate, she continued her prayer, "I hope Brother Shad will take his morning nap before I pick him up. I want him to be alert and pleasant when we spend time together today."

Blowing air over the hot liquid in her coffee cup, she sipped cautiously and stared out her kitchen window. Brother Shad's increased forgetfulness troubled her. A sigh emerged as she walked to the stove, stirred a pan of oatmeal and exclaimed in frustration, "He should call Tammy first, not me. His priorities seem scrambled. I shall tell his daughter of this situation. She *must* take more responsibility for his welfare."

Matti felt apprehensive for the old fellow while she ate her own breakfast. "You know, Lord, Brother Shad might leave me soon and go live with You. When we lived near each other in South Dakota towns long ago, I remember the good pastoral ministry that bonded our family lives together. But I know it won't be long before you come for him."

The thought prompted unresolved memories of her pastor husband. A tear warmed her cheek as it trickled toward her mouth. *Dan, we prayed and believed God for a miracle, even delayed your operation a few years ago until the last possible moment. We expected God's intervention. Instead, the colon cancer took you.*

"Dear, I still think of you every day. I can't let go. For 45 years we enjoyed a happy, healthy marriage. Now, our close friend, Brother Shad, feels the time of his home-going near. Matti daubed her

tears, cradled her head at the breakfast table, and prayed, "Lord, may Brother Shad's journey come another day. Please, not today."

LONELINESS INCREASES DESPONDENCY
MONDAY, MARCH 26, 7:30 A.M.

"Ooh -- lukewarm coffee again!" Brother Shad sputtered his displeasure. "Why can't this place serve hot coffee with my breakfast?" Sitting on the edge of his bed, he glared at his food tray. "I can eat corn and bran flakes, but eating ham mixed in a vegetable salad doesn't interest me. My Tammy would sympathize with me if I told her about this concoction on my plate. Best I lie down for another snooze."

Brother Shad's daughter, Tammy, relied upon Aunt Matti to assist and look in upon her father because of her recent years of care-giving experience with her own dad. She often expressed the feeling to her senior friend: "I believe time causes no effect on you. How do you do what you do? Paths you've trod, who can recount them all? You're a friend to folks nationwide!"

Aunt Matti would respond, "When people have a need, I try to be helpful."

Shad focused his eyes on Tammy's picture hung above his night stand. "Will you please come visit me today? Two weeks have passed since your last visit, when you gave me these new light-blue summer pajamas." (He no longer remembered she came to see him two days earlier.)

He looked again at her picture. "Tammy, I miss you, even though you call me every night. I do look forward to your night-time chit-chat. I even enjoy the recounting of the daily details of your library job. But, please, won't you come to see me again? A short visit would suffice."

After breakfast and with his morning nap completed, the aged pastor ambled outside along the sidewalk, careful not to stumble over uneven sections of cement in the first of his one-mile excursions around the apartment buildings and the City Center office complex. "O my, I forgot to wear my cap this morning. The heat of the sun may cause me sun-burn. But if I swing my arms back and forth, with these large beads of perspiration on my forehead, that may cool my head. Anyway, I'll lift them skyward and praise the Lord while I walk. I'll seek shelter under those trees near this section of my pathway."

On his walk, Brother Shad noticed the spring flowers not yet in full bloom, but then raised his gaze in wonderment, "How many years will these decapitated trees need to recover from the disfigurement of last winter's ice storms?"

He raised his hands in a prayer to God: "Lord, in Your sovereignty, have mercy on these towering giants. Please restore their branches. Jesus, they beautify our campus year around. The birds and little animals seek protection and food provided by these tall guardians."

Even the velvety deep-green carpet of grass filled with numerous insects eaten by families of robins and the overabundance of starlings now taking flight did not escape his observation. "Something spooked these birds. I'll keep my eyes open. I think there may be a den of coyote pups among the brush over by the lake, perhaps on the downhill side."

The breeze in the trees caused Brother Shad's attention to turn skyward. "I suppose those turkey buzzards and hawks enjoy high flights on the updrafts of spring rain clouds and they surely keep a watchful eye for a meal of field mice from the nearby woods."

His discerning eyes scanned the ground ahead on his persistent quest for dandelions, as on each day, for the object of his frustration. "Ah, a pesky dandelion." Red-faced, he spoke as if a new comer to the City Center stood by his side: "Duty demands I pull out every yellow-hatted green stem." His long-held hatred for this obnoxious weed dictated he pull up every one of these lawn-destroyers within sight. "Die, dandelions, die!" he gasped as he bent over, twisted and pulled up six tenaciously anchored roots.

A few minutes later in his walk, Brother Shad verbalized to his imagined companion, "Look at those geese. Nice. I see they like to eat grass on this slope. Hmm, 6, 8, 14 birds altogether. I presume they belong to the flock which took up residence on our new pond at the north side of the Center complex."

He hesitated under the trees along his pathway and sat down on a park bench to enjoy their graceful beauty. He loved the animals and birds. The creatures reminded him of his years growing up in Canada.

Brother Shad recalled a similar scene in his life at 15 years of age when he worked on his dad's farm, 40 miles north of the United States border in Saskatchewan. "Son," his dad called out from the horse barn, "don't forget to feed your flock of geese this morning."

The domestic birds greeted him with a chorus of raucous honks in anticipation of their breakfast of corn, which he hand-sprinkled near the windmill located at the top of the slope and at the side of the barnyard buildings.

"Come little ones," Shad had encouraged. "Eat your fill before the sun makes popcorn of your breakfast." On occasion, he would let the big birds eat kernels of corn out of his hand.

Their barnyard windmill pumped more than enough water needed to fill the horse tanks near the corral. Excess water flowed down the gentle slope and caused an abundant growth of grass covering a half acre of pastured hillside. Robins and doves found worms and bugs plentiful. The remainder of the overflow kept a cattle pond filled at the bottom of the hillside, not far from the beef cattle sheds.

His imaginary dialogue continued, "The geese loved to peck around the slope for greens and bugs. And the prairie winds kept the windmill pump busy in order that its water would meet the needs for our home, the milk cows, cattle, horses, chickens and geese."

Shad and his older sister, Michelle, a tall lady and close friend, drove the family work vehicle, a 1927 Chevrolet truck, to the Weyburn weekly market 15 miles away to sell chickens, eggs, butter, and geese.

Michelle, the only girl in their family and three years his senior, knew Shad best—born number six of the seven children. Both Shad and Michelle liked music; they both immersed themselves in the Word of God; both excelled in public speaking, and they both adored

Jesus.

One day on the way to market, they sang a loud and joyful duet to the melody of *Turn Your Eyes Upon Jesus*, a popular new song in their church. The chickens and geese harmonized with contented "clucks" and agreeable "honks," and often flapped their wings as if praising the Lord.

Their hymn sing with poultry accompaniment soon came to an abrupt halt. The gravel road with sandy bogs required their full attention. "Shad," Michelle suggested, "let's stop and throw a few shovels full of sand and gravel into these ruts. These washouts looked deep, even when I drove through here day before yesterday."

"Sounds good," Shad agreed as he stopped, then reached for a shovel stowed behind their seats. "We can save dad a repair bill. I'll continue our drive to market; you can navigate the return trip." Both teenagers mastered the 30-mile roundtrip obstacle course with enthusiasm and uncanny ability to avoid a high-center on hidden rocks or a bottom-out in a soupy quagmire.

At the City Center, Brother Shad's perceptive eyes set him apart from other residents. "Good afternoon, Ben. It looks like your work-out in the fitness room helps you walk better."

"Yes, Shad. I missed my regular times on the riding bike last week, because my son took me to Austin to visit my daughter and her family with four boys. Those young grandkids kept me involved in a host of activities—trips to the zoo, walks through museums, backyard baseball. I batted, they played 'chase grandpa's bad hits.'"

"Glad to see your family spends time with you, Ben, here and at their home. So, you became captain of the backyard ball club?"

"I thought our own two young ones were enough children to keep Myrtle and me busy in earlier years. But with my daughter's four active high schoolers—wow! I may need physical therapy for places in my body you'd never find listed in an anatomy book."

Shad's eyes brimmed with compassion as he placed a hand on Ben's shoulder, "You inspire me to continue my walks around the campus. See you at dinner tonight."

"Okay Shad, and be sure to dig up a handful of dandelions today for me, too."

Brother Shad continued his measured walk in the corridor near his room. "Hello, Sally. You look well today."

"Yes, Shad," she replied. "I received three roses from my grandson. It's nice to be remembered." With a welcome smile, the accomplished orator presented the appearance of a stately monarch whenever he met a resident or member of the nursing staff. "And your smile beams from ear to ear. Did something else happen to put you in such a good mood?"

"Yes, Shad. Mrs. 'P.' finished my perm five minutes ago. Do you like it?"

"Yes. Mrs. 'P.' molded it well to you facial features."

"I see that twinkle in your eyes. I accept your thoughtful observations, even though I believe you lie."

Shad's reply displayed his excellent skill and ability to communicate. "You mistake my feelings. For me, I like to see a well-kept woman like you, who holds her head up and who makes a habit of praising the Lord."

"Okay. I'll retract my previous comment. I believe you are a kind man."

"Sally, you continue to bless all of us in the Center with your gracious smile. And please believe me, your new hair-do complements your winsome personality."

"Mister Shadrach, I shall accept your well-intended comments this time. But next time we meet, be sure to tell me the truth. Please excuse me now. I must finish some paper work in my accounting cubicle for the boss."

Shad's quiet manners and soft-spoken voice impressed visitors when he greeted them with his large-boned handshake, fingers gnarled by his rough life as a Canadian farm boy and cowpoke accustomed to hard work on the grassland and grain prairie of the northern plains.

At 94 years of age, the cautious physical gait of this prayer warrior remained determined and calculated, ministry hardships of earlier decades forgotten. His thought processes, however, continued to develop evangelistic sermon outlines, a habit as natural to him as taking a walk each day around the City Center Retirement Home.

His dining room buddies knew better than to ask him, "Brother Shad do you suffer from the onset of Alzheimer's disease?"

A staff member would remind them, "Don't talk about it. Dementia frustrates him."

Thus, he often acted perplexed in conversations with friends or visitors and would remark, "My memory left me. Please forgive me. Tell me your name!"

At other times, his longtime ministerial associate, family friend, and former office accountant, Aunt Matti, in order to defuse his anxiety level, would exclaim: "Brother Shad, shall we go off campus for a chicken sandwich and coffee at Waldo's Bread Shop and Deli? Or shall we go over to Dolly's Ice Cream Parlor for a dish of your favorite mint chocolate-chip ice cream and coffee?"

"Let's go to Dolly's Ice Cream Parlor today," Brother Shad would reply. "Their ice cream melts in my mouth and they make good hot coffee." His periods of despondency at those moments and loneliness for his wife, Katy, long gone home to Jesus, would change to appreciation for another day to minister and praise the Lord.

The tactful table talk of Aunt Matti also brightened his day. "Brother Shad, let's go for a ride," or "May I drive you to church tomorrow morning?" When he found himself in ill health or in need of assistance, even in times of stressful predicaments, he first telephoned Aunt Matti before he called his daughter Tammy. Aunt Matti became his popular companion, his most concerned and trusted admirer since his wife died.

Charles T. Clauser

FAITHFUL AUNT MATTI

WEDNESDAY, MARCH 28, 8:00 A.M.

Each week, Matti's Friday morning hair appointments keep her brown hair neat and trim. She ate her lunch and dinner meals out, carefully monitoring her restaurant fare, that it did not add weight to her medium-sized torso.

If one judged by her demeanor and colorful clothes, she exuded the appearance of a mid-level executive. Her distinctive outfits trimmed with colorful brooches, pins, necklaces, or scarves accentuated her personality as a stylish business woman.

Her smooth stride, warm conversation, congenial manner, her knowledge of current events, and interest in the lives of others enhanced her desire to entertain missionary friends and long-time church family guests.

Her warm smile and pleasant laughter set people at ease as they observed and felt drawn into her preoccupation with living a life dedicated to Christian service.

Her house phone rang as she finished washing and drying the breakfast dishes. "Matti, I woke up this morning with a headache. I don't feel well. I'm dizzy. Matti, where am I?"

"In your room, Brother Shad, at the City Center. Did you eat any of your breakfast?"

"No. I'm woozy. I can't stand up. Please Matti, can you come and help me?"

"Brother Shad, sit down on your bed. Drink your orange juice and eat the ham slice on your tray. You need that protein. Please eat some of your breakfast. It will give you strength and make you feel better."

"I'm not hungry. I can't eat."

"Brother Shad, you will not get fat. Your body needs nourishment to survive. You *must* make yourself eat. The Lord needs your ministry. He needs your prayers and encouragement for the other residents and your inspiration for friends who come to visit you."

"Okay, Matti, I don't know what I would do without your help. I think I'm better already. Yesterday I walked seven miles. On one of my rounds, there were four little deer that crossed my path. They ran between the buildings and raced to a nearby grove of trees. The scene brought a breath of fresh air and brightened my day."

"Ooh, delightful. Now my friend, please drink your juice and eat a few bites of meat. You need that protein for strength. I will come to see you in two hours after you eat your breakfast and take your morning nap. If you feel better, we'll go order a chicken sandwich and some hot coffee at Waldo's."

"Okay. I shall attempt a few bites, just to please you, even though the food seems tasteless. I'm not hungry.

Brother Shad's sudden dizziness confused his ability to reason. "Did I just talk with Matti or was it my daughter Tammy? Why must I take another breath? My life is complete. My ministry doesn't amount to anything of consequence. I want to go be with You, Jesus.

"My daughter and my granddaughter Melody don't need me. They can manage life well on their own. Where am I? Whose picture is that on the wall? Why am I in this room? Didn't I eat breakfast already? I'm going to lie down and go back to sleep. Lord Jesus, please, send Your angels for me." He laid on his bed and looked up at the ceiling.

Bewildered, he spoke in short phrases: "Lord, You instructed Paul to tell us 'our citizenship is in heaven' (Philippians 3:20). I wait with anticipation for that event. I know You will transform my worn-out body to a new glorious body. Lord, with my ministry complete, I'm ready for You to take me home. For me, 'to die is gain' (Philippians 1:21). Jesus, please don't delay!"

CHAPTER TWO

SUDDEN ACCIDENTS SURMOUNTED

Bear one another's burdens.
Galatians 6:2

RESPONSIBIITY LEARNED ON THE FARM
WEDNESDAY, MARCH 28, 8:30 A.M.

PAINFUL MEMORIES of his childhood on the Canadian family farm bombarded Shad's mind. He tried to relax during his afterbreakfast naptime, but could not shake these recollections amid his groans and fidgeting. The tragedy of his brother's death overwhelmed his consciousness.

"Our heavy-duty John Deere tractor fell on my brother one mile west of our home because he did not follow safety rules." Shad verbalized his thoughts to a perceived unseen visitor. "Abner tried to plow on a sharp incline, sidewise to the slope of the hill, an act of poor judgment."

The scene flashed repeatedly like a rotating beacon across Brother Shad's mind. Frequent lapses like this one created unresolved despondency. "I can never forget that calamity. Abner did not return for the late afternoon chores. So Dad and I went to investigate. We didn't find him until near dark. We could see by a survey of the slope, he wanted to place more of the steep portion of the terrain under cultivation. We believed death came at once."

Innumerable times this horrid scene recurred in his mind. "I saw where the weight of the over-turned tractor wheels crushed his chest and head . . . a shocking sight. I must turn my head and close my eyes every time the image surfaces in my mind."

The sequence of events continued to roll through Brother Shad's mind, like a stuck phonograph needle. "We buried him two days later at the family grave site one-half mile north of the horse shed, among a dozen cottonwood trees watered by a small spring."

Shad continued his half-mumbled intermittent conversation. "Dad asked me to say a prayer at the funeral. Abner, a big guy, often took care of me and taught me how to succeed in farm work. I tried my best at Dad's suggestion to write a couple of sentences about Abner. The Lord helped me compose five sentences of appreciation."

Brother Shad shed a tear and prayed: "Lord, I still don't understand why that casualty happened. The ground may have been wet and a wheel may have sunk into a soft spot. Or perhaps the tractor wheel dropped into the edge of a badger hole. But I believe You have my brother Abner with You in heaven. I miss him, we all miss him. He treated me well, took me under his arm, taught me meaningful shortcuts in our ranch work. Lord, please keep. . . ."

Tears moistened his cheeks as he lay on his bed unable to sleep. Abner's death and the emotion of the funeral hit him hard. He sobbed: "My stomach hurt, my shoulders ached, I leaned against Mom for strength and support throughout the funeral."

He spoke again to the imaginary person he felt stood beside his bed and related to his unseen guest how his dad with tear-moistened cheeks finished the tribute to Abner: "Jesus, You gave us this robust, hardworking young man. We give thanks. You came into his life on Easter, five years ago and gave him new life.

"Thank You, Lord. We shared family life together for several years. He blessed our family. We know he came from dust and to dust he returned. His eternal soul rests in Your hand. Therefore, I know we shall see him and rejoice on that great reunion day in heaven."

Dad Milburn surprised Shad with this show of emotion. The committal service ended amid tears and sorrowful "amens." Dad Milburn had planned for Abner, a capable young man, to take over the ranch operation in future days. But with Abner dead at age 18, the thought crossed young Shad's mind: *The day may soon come when this responsibility will rest upon my shoulders.*

GRANDPA MILBURN'S DEATH

Sleep continued to evade Brother Shad. He tossed, he squirmed, he rolled both ways in his narrow bed, he lay on his back, and rolled onto his stomach, all in an attempt to relax his tense muscles. He fought the dizziness and unsettledness that bombarded his consciousness. Soon, another unpleasant memory surfaced from his early life on the farm. He started a new monologue. His agitation grew.

"Our family buried Grandpa Milburn under the same cottonwood trees three years before Abner's death. Grandpa froze to death in the middle of a vicious January three-day snow and ice storm that killed several cattle in our family herd. He went out to the feedlot with Dad and two of the older boys to help rescue all the cattle possible whose noses and eyes had frozen shut."

These memories, even now, chilled Brother Shad's arms and face when he remembered the extreme cold on the second day of that winter storm. "That event," he muttered, believing his companion nearby, "happened in seconds. Grandpa secured himself with a rope tied to the corner of the shed, but the line broke when some of the heifers moved in behind him near the shed to seek shelter from the full force of the ice and snow mixture.

"The broken line caused him to fall into a snow bank. He never found his way back to our barn in that harsh weather, just 50 feet away. Dad and David, my second eldest brother, found him two days later after the storm abated, head down in a snow bank.

"I miss Grandpa Milburn. All the family missed him, a wonderful, gentle man." Brother Shad continued his dialogue with his imaginary cohort. "I miss him because we played checkers together and that winter he started to teach me the game of chess."

Deep sleep continued to elude Brother Shad throughout his morning nap time. His stressed emotional state caused the retired minister's mind to roam again through memories of teen years at their Canadian farm.

This time, summer, eight years later, "The sun peeked through the elm tree leaves outside my bedroom window. It cast playful daybreak shadows on the wall beside my bunk bed. My eyes opened, half mast, and I heard the milk cows bellow for their breakfast. A morning dove cooed on top of the garage. I turned to look at the clock—5 a.m. I knew it was time to arise and start the morning chores.

"'Thank you, Lord, for the fine night's sleep.' I touched my younger brother Aaron who slept in the upper bunk. 'Aaron, time to wake up.'

"Four years younger than me, Aaron grasped details and procedures of the farm operation with enthusiasm. A bright boy, he loved animals, books, and the opportunity to learn about nature.

"Come on, Aaron, let's go check the cows. Today, we leave at 7:30 for school. Michelle will confer with the principal about her senior graduation on Friday afternoon. She plans to play piano for the ceremony and accompany the girl's trio. Mom made her a new dress and Dad said we will all attend her special event."

"Shad, tell Mom I need five more minutes sleep."

"No, Aaron." Shad spoke with gentle authority, "We must check the livestock in the corral and see that the hired men milk the cows. Dad said we should remember to take two dozen eggs with us today for your teacher, Miss Henry."

The cool weather tempted both boys to sleep in. But Shad, at age fifteen, and now the foreman for the Milburn Ranch, exercised new responsibilities and a trust he dare not break. He loved his father, felt honored to receive the burden for these important tasks, and devoted all his free time not set aside for school activities to the successful supervision of the ranch enterprise.

Reminiscences rolled on through Shad's mind. The flash back this time involved Dad Milburn, who coached young Shad each day in leadership skills. These sessions took place in the horse barn, near the pigpen, or in the family living room

"Shad, we must relate well with people as well as with animals. If we show concern for the welfare of our hired men, they will give us a full day of work. Similarly, if we don't drive the horses too hard, but give them regular rest breaks, they will plow a field without hesitation and with no frothing at the mouth.

"Keep a sharp eye out," his dad cautioned, "for changes in weather conditions. Adverse weather may affect the animal's behavior or the safety of the hired men."

Instruction in those living room sessions dealt with grain market trends—buy, sell, hold, and basic record keeping. Shad's monologue rolled on. "Dad proved himself a skillful financier, and thrifty even when cash was in short supply. He passed management tips on to me each day as I strove to process his advice and instruction.

"My will to persevere as foreman took precedence over my desire to remain catcher of the Weyburn High School baseball team. Those leadership skills I learned while in my teens served well in my soon-to-begin ministerial career."

MATTI WILL COME
WEDNESDAY, MARCH 28, 10:00 A.M.

At last, sleep quieted his mind and body. But within minutes, Shad opened wide his eyes in a surprised expression. In desperation he looked at the dresser clock and talked out loud to himself. "I must shave and dress. I know Matti will come in fifteen minutes. I shall enjoy a drive away from campus and the opportunity to catch a change of scenery. 'Thank you, Lord, for waking me.'"

On her way, Matti stopped for a red light on Dakota Street, halfway to the retirement community. Her active mind forgot about her driving requirements. She recalled an event of World War II, May 15, 1945, on the day of her high school graduation.

Thoughts of her classmate and sweetheart Zeke surfaced. "If that kamikaze pilot had not hit the deck of your aircraft carrier, you would have lived. I wonder what paths our lives would have followed had we married? I loved you and I know you loved me."

Blatt! Blatt!

Impatient drivers broke her reverie with the sounds of strident horns. She spun her wheels to clear the intersection. Her mind instantly concentrated on the purpose for her drive to the City Center. In a determined manner, she slapped the steering wheel with the palm of her hand and spoke to the car in the lane ahead. "I must stop at McDonalds and buy a cup of coffee for Brother Shad. He will expect it."

She arrived in the Center at 10:10 a.m., and brought Brother Shad the cup of steaming black liquid. "Thank you. I recognized the click of your heels on the tiled corridor. Matti. You're an angel!" He cradled the warm Styrofoam cup in his hands, then looked in despair at the woman who wore the red blouse and green knit vest, seated in his room.

"I should know her. Why did she come into my room? . . . In moments, his memory returned, "I don't think I'm up to a ride out for a chicken sandwich. I must lie down again. Matti, what happened to me?"

"You look fine, Brother Shad. Lie down and rest. I'll sit in your chair until you go to sleep. By afternoon, we can go out for a snack, maybe a taco or some ice cream. Until then, sleep well, but first, take another sip or two of your coffee."

The previous night, Matti had worked late. The house clock on her fireplace mantel chimed 2:30 a.m. as she finished her e-mail correspondence and birthday cards. She slept hard for the next few hours, still exhausted when Brother Shad called earlier, not too attentive or pleasant in her response.

Now, she sat relaxed in Brother Shad's dilapidated lounge chair, closed her eyes, kicked off her shoes, and reflected upon their five decades of association. *How can anyone plumb the depth of this knowledgeable student of the Bible, a man accustomed to reading two books of the Bible every day? An expositor who preached on five continents during seventy-five years of ministry? A gentleman whose family and former associates still hold him in high esteem?*

Nevertheless, I must use this opportunity to pray for my family, since my prayer time fell short this morning. She prayed for different people and situations both she and Brother Shad had known over the years, and interceded first for him. "Lord, please continue Your protection for Brother Shad. Keep him safe in your right hand.

"Empower his daughter Tammy in her library work. May she keep a sweet smile on her face and humor in her interaction with people, above all, with the children. May her daughter Melody, learn to play the oboe well. Help that young girl practice with diligence each day. And, Lord, I ask that you keep the City Center staff focused on their responsibilities."

She remembered how Brother Shad despised even the sight of a dandelion. Barely audible came her words: "Dear Lord, I pray Brother Shad shall remember to wear his cap next time he goes out for a walk. If he yanks out several dandelions, he might bring on a heat stroke on these hot spring days. Lord, You know he doesn't think in rational ways anymore. Please keep Your hand of protection on him."

She drifted in and out of sleep because of her short night of rest, but she tried her best to continue in earnest prayer for her aged friend and his family. The stoplight incident an hour earlier left Aunt Matti unnerved. *What if I had fallen asleep at the wheel?* Her mind blocked out the possible reality and ramifications of such an accident.

Instead, her thoughts drifted back to 1939, western South Dakota, cow country, her farm home.

Matti saw herself at age 14 and upset. Her father and mother, the Hendersons, both new Christians, gave up their farm life and moved to Ingrid's Well, a nearby town, to begin a new Pentecostal preaching career. She had grown up on the family farm, loved the out-of-doors, learned to milk cows, enjoyed the animals, even practiced the piano under the tutelage of her father in order to play in their church services.

The trauma of the move to her father's first pastorate overwhelmed her. He told her, "I taught you to play piano; you are our church pianist; you *must* come with us." She understood her father's orders and realized the Henderson clan were too poor for her to attend high school.

"Someday," she affirmed through grinding teeth, *"I shall earn sufficient funds and attain the appropriate personal skills to live by myself. Until then, I know God will provide for my high school education."*

And the day after the Henderson family arrived in town, Mister Orvis McNeal, the postmaster for the small village of Ingrid's Well, talked with Aunt Matti's father and stated his need. "My wife Gloria, an invalid for five years, suffers from polio. She can no longer perform basic activities in our home. She cannot cook, garden, or do housework.

"She needs assistance each day in order to move from her bed to a chair. A high school girl, who assisted me with home care for my wife, left three days ago to attend nursing school in Sioux Falls.

"I need a caregiver today. Reverend Henderson, would your daughter Matilda consider the job? I will provide room and board, pay her high school expenses, and give her $2.50 per week. In return, she will live in our home, cook our meals, clean the house, and care for the needs of my wife. We have a boy, Bryce, almost seven years old, ready to enter second grade."

GLORIA'S CAREGIVER

Matti's reminiscences continued as she drifted in and out of sleep. "I accept the offer, Dad. It means I can attend my freshman year at Ingrid's Well High School."

"Your assignment starts tomorrow morning at 7:00 a.m.," Reverend Henderson cracked a big smile on his face as he quoted the postmaster. Then placed his arm around her shoulder in a hug, "Do your best, Matti. Your Mom and I are proud of you."

The next morning Mister McNeal introduced Matti to Gloria and Bryce. "Your first assignment—cook a breakfast of sausage, fried potatoes and sliced tomatoes, served with milk and coffee." Matti didn't know whether to hide or run, fake it or trust in the Lord.

Mister McNeal, a patient man, explained: "Matti, I know it will take time to learn our routine. Allow me to guide you each day, and explain new situations to you in the acquiring of new household and care-giving skills."

The conversations at meal times in the McNeal home included a variety of topics. Mrs. McNeal encouraged her husband's discussion. Matti felt like she was sitting in a civics class, some days a history class, or drinking a soda at the local variety store. Meal times in the McNeal home were never dull.

The conversations covered gossip, local news, or current events of national interest. For example, the year 1939 proved a difficult economic time for South Dakotans as President Roosevelt instituted the Work Projects Administration (WPA).

These discussions brought world issues right to the McNeal's dinner table. They often reviewed how the United States economy struggled to get back on its feet from the recession experienced in recent years, while the mid-Western states sought solvency after the near ruin from the recent long-term drought. Rumbles about a possible World War II caught the attention of mid-Western cattlemen and farmers as well as those in McNeal household.

Matti's duties included not only household chores and the preparation of meals, but managing a devious seven-year-old boy who often faked imaginary pain, pretended sickness, and said: "I don't want to go to school." His reluctance tested Matti's ingenuity for obtaining his compliance.

Matti told Brother Shad in later years, "I would walk over a half mile to school each day, study my lessons, and care for Gloria in the McNeal home. I found relief in prayer for each stressful situation. 'Lord, without Your strength and guidance, I cannot complete my responsibilities today. But only by Your grace, can I maintain my grades, because I arrive late for school on many days.'"

One month after her employment began, Mr. McNeal said to Matti: "Here are the keys to our car. Learn to drive it." Surprised, Matti did not know how to react to his request. She had only watched her boss drive. Therefore, she knew what knobs he turned and pushed as he prepared to start or stop the car, a 1937 Model A Ford touring car.

"Jesus," she said, "please help me reign in this special team of horses." With the Lord's help, plus one week's experience of frantic starts and stops on the street in front of the McNeal home, she felt confident to say to Mrs. McNeal, "Let's go for a ride."

Gloria enjoyed those afternoon tours around the small farming community, which commenced when Matti arrived home after school. Both ladies enjoyed the ride. But Matti always knew when to say, "Mrs. McNeal, I believe we should return home. I must prepare dinner."

When Matti's dad learned that she drove the McNeal's car, he expressed horror, "Matti, please use caution. You might wreck the vehicle and endanger Mrs. McNeal."

Matti consoled her dad by saying, "A person can receive a driver's license at age 13, and Mr. McNeal arranged for me to receive my license without problems or restrictions."

In the coldest of winter weather and in periods of bad storms, Mr. McNeal would say: "Matti you may drive our car to and from school today."

"Matti," Brother Shad interrupted her daydreams as the lunch bell sounded by the nursing station. "Will you please help me walk to the dining room? My three buddies expect me to eat lunch with them. We always share the same table. My head feels better, and I feel hungry."

On the slow march to the dining room, he commented to Matti, "I hope my daughter will come visit me this afternoon."

CHAPTER THREE

SUPPRESSED ANGER EXPLODES

He who is slow to wrath has great understanding.
Psalm 14:29

AN INVITATION TO AN ICE CREAM PARTY
THURSDAY, MARCH 29, 10:00 A.M.

MATTI GREETED BROTHER SHAD in his room at the City Center with a slight curtsey and a cheery, "You called, Sir? What time does your watch say? Does it indicate this morning a good occasion for us to pop over to Dolly's Ice Cream Parlor for some mint chocolate-chip ice cream and a cup of coffee?"

Looking up at her with a big smile on his face, he shook her hand. "Matti, you read my thoughts," he said, laying his open Bible on the table near his chair. "I'll accompany you with pleasure this morning, and I believe we may find ample time to accomplish both activities before lunch today." Then, he added with a frown, "You know, today marks the 11th anniversary of my wife Katy's death."

"Yes, Brother Shad, I remember." She touched his arm lightly and sat down on the chair near his. Matti recalled, "She treated me as a close friend, ever since our first association together in the kitchen and dining room at our camp meetings 50 years ago. I knew you would think of her, and I knew you would appreciate company today."

"I miss her. I love her yet, just like when we last lived together. Every year on this day I feel depressed." He sniffed and blew his nose. "If she lived today, our celebration would mark 68 joyous years together, years of harmony and family fulfillment."

"You two experienced a blessed life together." Matti pointed to his wedding picture on the wall directly in front of his vision as he sat in his chair. "How the Lord used you both in ministry amazes me. Both of you demonstrated a remarkable partnership in your pastorates. And I believe you served well at our district office." She tried to divert his attention to other events in his life. "You even exhibited exceptional competency in your ministry as a national representative for our fellowship."

"I know you want to encourage me, Matti." Shad inhaled deeply and placed his hands behind his head. "God blessed me in every position He placed me. In addition, I can say He gave me a wonderful daughter and topped my ministry with abundant domestic and foreign travel."

His smile became a scowl. "I didn't deserve any of those certificates and plaques given me by the brothers at the central office. I give all the glory to Jesus."

"Brother Shad, I see you feel better, since we started to talk. I believe you feel strong enough and might be interested in a little treat at Dolly's."

"Yes, Matti, Let's go," he smiled, stood up, and adjusted his shirt collar. "Your presence brightens my day. I will enjoy it more because of the beautiful day and the flowers in bloom."

"The morning coolness left a bit of dew on the ground. Bring your sweater," Matti urged as she buttoned her own sweater. "Sometimes the air conditioner at the ice cream shop tends to chill a person. Instead, we need heat today. I'll wear my wool sweater inside Dolly's for a light cover over my shoulders."

After a slow walk to the parking lot, he settled down into the front seat, buckled his seat belt and with a grin, observed: "The geese from our pond came again to eat insects on the slope beyond your car. Look at them, busy on the bug detail for breakfast in the grass, while the squirrels forage last year's seeds for their meal." Contented, Brother Shad waved his hand and commented, "I enjoy the presence of wildlife at the Center."

Matti wrinkled her nose. "I must say, I find them quite messy. I hope they stay on the slope." And pointing her bobbing finger near his face, admonished, "I don't want to give my shoes a special clean up and shine every time I come see you."

Brother Shad raised a hand toward the birds and prayed: "You geese, please return each day. You give joy to the children who play in the front yards of nearby homes and my friends who reside in the assisted-living quarters. . . ."

Aunt Matti appeared not to hear him as she focused her attention on the road conditions at the Center. She drove past several cars parked near the chapel, where occupants prepared to attend the funeral of a recently deceased resident. She didn't know the person, but felt: *I want to take Brother Shad away from this scene as soon as possible so he will forget his depression over his deceased wife.*

"Watch your step, Brother Shad. This small curb at the edge of the sidewalk entrance looks tricky. I wish they would paint it yellow. It would help identify the difference in height. I stumbled here once myself. Oops! Careful, Brother Shad. If you fall, I can't help you up. You weigh too much for me to pick up."

"Thanks for the assistance, Matti. You rescued me again."

Inside the front door, Matti motioned to her friend. "Let's sit in this booth. While you secure the booth, I'll order for us."

"Sounds good, Matti. I'll take my usual, please."

As Aunt Matti walked toward the counter to place their order, a familiar senior-citizen, Sandra, beckoned to her in spite of a raspy, asthmatic voice. "Hi Matti! I can't count the years since we last saw you." She wheezed, "Please bring Brother Shad over and join us. We finished Sid's medical appointment earlier at the clinic. Had a good report for his cholesterol and broken ankle. Thought we'd come and celebrate a bit before we headed home."

"Okay, Sandra. I believe, not years, but ages have vanished since we last connected. First, let me place our order, then I'll bring Brother Shad. I know he'll enjoy our contact again. I remember," her hand slapped her forehead, "I last saw you—oh, more than two years ago. I think you moved out to Bear Lake. Thirty minutes of chit-chat will only start our catch up of family news."

In minutes, the four sat together. Matti made the introductions, "Brother Shad, shake hands with my dear friends from Bear Lake. Sid and Sandra, who used to pastor in South Dakota over at Stirrup, not too far from Dan and me."

"Friends, I'm happy to meet you," he responded, assuming his stance as an accomplished orator and stately monarch.

"Reverend Shad, we first met you thirty years ago at the Heartstone Campground. You spoke for both morning and evening services." Reverend Sid, a small man in stature, talked fast, seldom stopping to breathe. He listed the salient points of speaker Shad's series for the Sermon on the Mount and recalled, "Brother Shad spoke for five days with Holy Spirit inspiration in those meetings, quite boldly I must say. The services left a definite impact upon my ministry."

"Stop, please, Brother Sid." Shad raised his hands in protest. "You make me feel embarrassed by emphasizing my style. In any series of messages or in a single sermon, we must always promote

Jesus, not ourselves. He receives the preeminence." Shad's rapid finger moments filled the air. "People need to see Jesus in us, not our pretty ways of a presentation."

"Oh, please excuse me, Brother Shad," Sid's hands reached to the sky, his upper body fell backward against the booth backrest. "I didn't mean any offense, sir. However, after all these years, the thrust of your messages at camp never left me. Many young people made decisions that year to follow Jesus, even several adults." He spoke slowly and softly to reassure Brother Shad of his sincerity. "I remember the Spirit of God made it a glorious camp meeting."

"Your apology accepted, Brother Sid." Shad made himself relax and quiet down. "Perhaps my reaction sounded too harsh. Still," he declared, "Jesus must occupy first place in every aspect of our lives. He reigns over people and all events."

"Sandra," Aunt Matti asked during the momentary hesitation in the conversation, "did your two boys finish college?"

"Yes," she replied, her plump body and asthma caused extended conversation difficult. "Both live in the Twin Cities area of Minnesota. Mike practices medicine, and Matthew works as an electrical engineer. Mike's three children keep their grade school teachers busy; Matthew's twin girls show talent in their high school creative writing and debate classes. Both families attend active, vibrant churches. I feel blessed."

"The little guys I recall," Matti looked into the distance for a moment and then back at Sandra, "loved basketball and choir when

Dan and I saw you twenty-one years ago in Chamberlain. They give you much happiness, don't they?"

The delightful interchange about family events, grandchildren's activities, current home locations, and renewed friendship continued well through the noon hour. Brother Shad could not remember many details of recent years, but did express a vague remembrance of some names and places mentioned. "Sid, I'm sorry. Those names escape me." His frustration level, agitation and anxiety caused Matti to recognize his lack of food. He needed a protein snack to relieve his hypoglycemic symptoms.

Perceptive to his mood, manner of speech, and need for solid food, Matti said, "Brother Shad, I think it time for us to go somewhere for our dinner. Sandra, Sid—dear friends, will you excuse us, please? Brother Shad's blood sugar hit bottom. We must put regular food in him. But, let's not allow another twenty-one years or even two to pass by before our next rendezvous. Okay?"

"Yes, Matti. Please call me soon."

"Come, Brother Shad. I know a good place to eat nearby with ready food, a buffet with short lines and immediate service. My stomach started to gurgle with hunger. I think I hear your stomach bubbling, too."

"My body tells me it needs food. Good-bye, dear friends. You made my day complete with this talk of twenty- and thirty-year old memories." Shad stood up to leave, but inquired respectively, "Uh . . . please, tell me your names again."

Charles T. Clauser

A SPRING AFTERNOON COLOR TOUR
SATURDAY, MARCH 31, 2:00 P.M.

"Let's go for an afternoon drive, Brother Shad." Several spring flowers bloomed this week with a variety of gorgeous colors. The drive will reinvigorate you. What do you say we go for a ride in the country?" Aunt Matti knew a countryside drive, a favorite pastime of the old gentleman, would cheer his disposition.

"I'll put on my shoes, Matti. Tell me the temperature. Will I need a light jacket?"

"The weather report on TV this morning said 72 degrees this afternoon with no rain clouds in sight. I foresee a perfect day for fresh air and a bit of sunshine. Bring your jacket. We might go into a restaurant later for cherry pie a la mode."

"Please, no blackberry pie because of seeds and my loose dentures," he scowled. "But I would not hesitate, however, to sink my teeth into a piece of pumpkin pie." His frown turned into a gigantic smile, "Of course, with a big dip of my favorite ice cream."

"What would you savor today, my friend?"

"Mint chocolate chip. But plain vanilla would taste good on pumpkin pie. Tell me your favorite flavor of ice cream, Matti."

"Banana pecan yogurt," she smacked her lips. He could hear her croon "Yum-Yum" as she exited his room to go out for the car.

Their color tour proceeded east through city subdivisions, away from busy roads, past beautiful neighborhood garden patches filled with iris, lilac bushes, tulips, and groups of yellow jonquils.

Brother Shad's Dandelions

Both friends expressed appreciation to God. "I feel I could write a book," Bother Shad beamed, "about the beauty of these carpets of green grass adorned with groves of oak, elm, and pine trees." He breathed deeply, "I love the spring aroma of new blossoms and fields of clover."

"Peaceful and delightful," Matti agreed as she soaked up the warmth of the spring afternoon sun. "The open windows of my car will allow a gentle breeze in, also, the delicious smells of the new-mown grass, the pink dogwood trees, and the purple hyacinths. Let's sit with the engine turned off and let God speak to us through His magnificent creation."

"And we can lift our hearts," Brother Shad nodded his head, "in reference to the Master Gardener. I can feel His presence and sense His care for everything around us by the way the animals and birds eat with contentment."

A pair of cardinals conversed between a spruce and a red cedar tree. Two hummingbirds enjoyed the nectar of a bird feeder placed low to the ground near a bed of peach-colored peonies and located close to a large front window of a dark-red brick home nearby. The serenity of this quiet time encouraged both senior citizens to bask in the warmth of the afternoon sun and listen to the sounds of the neighborhood.

Angry squirrels fought over nuts at the base of a large pine tree. Talkative geese honked at each other over a grassy feeding area near a small farm pond. Loud-voiced crows cawed, who knows why, in close-by treetops. And the smell of cherry tree blossoms in a small roadside orchard emitted a fragrance that tantalized pollinating bees.

Matti declared: "I forget the problems associated with our town activities when I see nature in this glorious display of life. The drive today gives me much pleasure. Like you, Brother Shad, I feel immense satisfaction when I look at God's beauty. We are blessed to live under the care of a great Creator."

Matti started the engine and continued outbound on their spring-colors tour. As she drove, they left the community behind, wound through narrow country roads, meandered up gentle hillsides and crossed over shallow valleys. They passed by pastoral scenes of wild turkeys and herds of beef cattle at rest in the warm afternoon sun.

The farm scenes proved therapeutic to both seniors. They stopped a second time, absorbed in the splendor of well-fed farm animals. Relaxed in spirit by the beauty of ankle-high corn fields, and the orderliness of well-tended vegetable gardens, Farmer Shad indulged in a nap.

Thirty minutes later, Aunt Matti glanced over at Brother Shad, awakened him, and suggested in her mild voice: "What say we go to Dolly's for an ice cream snack?"

"Humph!" he gasped for air. "What did you say Matti? Guess I dozed for a moment amid this spectacular scenery. Can't remember when I so enjoyed an afternoon in the countryside."

"I think we should head toward Dolly's. Any objections?"

"None. Let's go . . . *"Matti, watch out, that truck,"* Brother Shad shouted. *"It may side-swipe us!"*

At the same moment, Matti pushed hard on the brakes and sent them bouncing into the windshield. The car came to an abrupt stop one foot from a steep embankment. "Sorry, I swerved to the right in order to miss that farm truck as it careened around us. I wanted to avoid a collision with it. Praise the Lord, we didn't spin around and drop off into that ravine. My heart feels ready to explode! Brother Shad, do you feel okay?"

"I think I'm okay, Matti. But my glasses fell off. Can you help me find them? Ah, here they are, nestled in the jacket on my lap. Thank God, the lenses appear intact, no bent rim. Matti, how about you? You okay?"

"Yes, I think so. Whew! Close call. But, I feel a slight pain in my ribs. Guess I hit my left side on the steering wheel or maybe the dash board when I veered right and stopped on the edge. Ouch! I need to breathe slowly. Mmm. I must take small breaths for awhile. This near-crash shook me up!"

"I feel a bit better," Brother Shad said. "Let me pray for us. We'll ask the Lord to touch you and take away the cause of the pain in your ribs."

"Yes, please."

"'Father, we give You thanks for our safety. We thank You for Your protection from the big ravine, which our car did not flip over. You kept us alive, Lord. Please heal Matti's ache in her side. Minister good health to her we pray. Take away the pain. Cause everything in her side to return to normal.

"And we thank You for answering our prayer. Oh yes, Lord, we lift up to You the driver of that truck who almost wrecked both vehicles just minutes ago. Please keep Your hand on him and protect all vehicles and persons on the road wherever he may drive. In Jesus' name, I pray. Amen.'"

"Thank you, Brother Shad. I feel better. 'Thank You, Lord, for Your physical touch.' I'll proceed with caution on our return to town."

As they began the ascent up the last slope two miles east of town, Matti exclaimed: "Three teenagers died in a two-car wreck at this exact location three months ago. The sheriff called it a passing type of accident. The driver crossed over a double yellow line, on this same slope, but with a wet road. The driver of one car thought he could pass the other vehicle before the top of the hill. Only one maimed young person survived. After more than two months in the hospital, the doctors released her."

Her composure rattled, emotions raw, Matti turned on the car radio. "Brother Shad, please turn to KWTJ, our local Christian station. My watch says 3:30, time for the mid-afternoon news."

As he tuned in the station, the announcer reported with enthusiasm, "the local Blackwater High School baseball team won their game, nine to five. But ladies and gentlemen," the announcer hesitated and spoke with measured words, a tinge of dread in his voice . . . .

"A terrible truck accident occurred out on County Road 5, only minutes before our scheduled newscast. The driver and a passenger, both males, missed a curve. Both were killed after their truck flipped over and dropped into a 20-foot narrow ravine. In the rescue effort, the Blackwater City Sheriff reported, beer bottles lay scattered on the floor and on the seat beside the two young men."

The newscast continued "A driver of an oncoming car reported: 'had we arrived at that corner three seconds sooner, we might have plummeted over the cliff, too. We slowed down and pulled over to the shoulder to avoid an accident. The driver of the truck sped by us at a high rate near a curve, then veered in erratic movements across the road before he plunged over the cliff.'"

Matti slowed down, stopped the car, and looked at her companion: "Brother Shad," her tears flowed obscuring her vision, "only God kept us from a flight into that ravine. I feel the truck which passed us not more than twenty minutes ago, which they reported rolled off the road. It's the same one. What a horrible way to end one's life. I," she covered her eyes, hands shaking, "I need a cup of coffee."

The newscast concluded with one more item of concern about the truck accident. "Sheriff Bing released the identity of both young men: The driver, Chad Holmes, 18-year-old son of Pastor Chink Holmes of the Blackwater Community Church, and Pinky Hadson, his passenger and 18-year-old son of Gibb Hadson, superintendent of the Blackwater Regional School District. Both boys, members of Blackwater High School played in the baseball game this afternoon.

Both boys left the stadium an hour earlier, right after the final inning. Listen to our 6:00 p.m. newscast for more details."

Click!

Brother Shad turned off the radio. "I've heard enough of sorrowful events today and in my lifetime. I wanted to remember the beautiful farm lands and gorgeous scenery we saw this afternoon. Matti, will you take me home? This bad news makes me weary and depressed. Those two boys had much to live for with energy and talent to share with others.

"They could have served Jesus with all their vitality. I pray they did know the saving grace of Jesus. I don't feel good, and to think we missed death by a tire width, almost pushed off the road, and over a cliff. Please take me to the Center. I must lie down." "Okay, my friend. First, however, we shall make a stop for coffee. I'm still quite shaky. Let me dry my eyes before we continue our ride back to town. Our great afternoon excursion has turned sour.

"I know the parents of both boys. May God have mercy on their families."

PART TWO

SUMMER: CHANGES TO A NEW LIFESTYLE

*The steps of a good man are ordered by
the LORD, And He delights in his way.
Though he fall, he shall not be utterly cast
down, For the LORD upholds him with
His hand.*
Psalm 37:23, 24

CHAPTER FOUR

STEWARDSHIP SETTLES AGE DIFFERENCES

We have the mind of Christ.
Corinthians 1 2:16

MEMORY RETENTION CHALLENGED
TUESDAY, JUNE 26, 3:00 P.M.

SHAD MUMBLED, DISGRUNTLED and frustrated as he arose from his afternoon nap, "Lord, I see You kept me here." He tottered to his worn lounge chair, plopped down on its ripped seat cushion, and cast a disparaging look out his window hoping to see a robin by the pool. As he looked back to pick his Bible, one of his young pastor friends, Chris Carpenter, knocked and waited for an invitation to step into the room.

"Hi, Brother Shad," he said in reply to the aging pastor's welcome hand motion. "I wanted to talk with you again before you go out for a walk to yank out more dandelions."

"Granted Chris, let's give the Bible priority. Those pesky weeds can wait. I'll destroy twice as many next time I walk around our campus." Evident to each man, they both sought a deeper saturation of the Word in their lives."

"I enjoy our discussions," Brother Shad affirmed as he opened his Bible to the book of Luke, "because we focus on the Word of God." For example, I studied Luke 1:32 throughout this last year. Chris, the passage emphasizes Christ: 'He will be great, and will be called the Son of the Highest.'

"The word *great* in this verse fascinates me," Brother Shad spoke with enthusiasm, "and I read this emphasis elsewhere in Gospel passages. The context begins in Luke 1:26. The angel Gabriel informs Mary she has found 'favor with God' and 'shall bring forth a Son . . . Jesus.' In the word *great*," Brother Shad said, "*G* declares He shall be great because He remains forever God."

His comments turned into preaching. "*R* indicates He stands for the revelation of God, Jesus Christ. *E* signifies Emmanuel, God with us. *A* embodies atonement, how He gave His life on the Cross for me. *T* constitutes truth. 'He is the way, the truth and the life' (John 14:6). If you want truth, look to Jesus. Jesus called me out of sin. He spoke to my heart, made me a child of God, an heir of the King."

Chris nodded his head in agreement and replied before Shad could comment further. "I like your acrostic. These letters demonstrate powerful points for our understanding of salvation: God, Jesus Revealed, Emmanuel, Atonement, and Truth. Brother Shad, I share your love for evangelism and eternal truths. Your ability to extract the salient points in a passage like this impresses me. Your mind discerns truth in each line. Did you ever develop these thoughts into a tract?"

"No. But I immerse myself each day in Bible reading, at least 20 chapters per day, no matter which books of the Bible I choose to read."

A dinner bell sounded the call for supper. It disallowed further discussion of these spiritual precepts. Both men stood up. Bother Shad concluded Chris' visitation with a warm request: "Please come again Brother Carpenter. I want to hear your thoughts about the word *great*."

"Okay. I shall prepare for our next visit. Eat well, Brother Shad." Chris exited Brother Shad's room after a handshake, and walked down the corridor humming *Jesus is the sweetest name I know*.

Brother Shad washed his hands and face in preparation for supper, glanced into his bathroom mirror, noted the reflection of pictures and citations on the wall behind himself. His eyes focused on the framed picture of his honorary doctor of divinity degree awarded in 1978.

With face moist, hands not yet dry, he turned around. His eyes stopped this time on a framed newspaper clipping which portrayed himself with his wife Katy. Both stood behind a two-foot high, 50th-year wedding anniversary cake.

"Katy, oh my Katy," he recalled with tearful eyes. "Your friends described you as sweet, a homebody type, a personable lady. In our ministry together, you preached and went on visitation with me. My Precious One, people felt comfortable with you and delighted in your sense of humor. I appreciated the fact you adapted yourself to my mannerisms each day and everywhere we ministered. I miss you, my Dear. Oh, the good times we enjoyed together."

During their South Dakota camp meetings, Katy would coordinate the dining room preparations and services. Like her husband, she exerted good leadership, and earned the status of a popular person among the pastoral families. She consented to play piano or accordion on occasion, but sang with reluctance, even though she performed with a crystal-clear and mellow alto voice.

"Katy, my love, I hope to join you before long." Brother Shad caressed the framed picture of their 50th celebration. He gave no attention to the family portraits, snapshots of friends or professional citations, which covered every bit of space on the walls in his one-room home at the Center. Only one other picture mattered to him, beside the one of their 50th anniversary, the framed words behind his ramshackle chair which affirmed: "Jesus Never Fails!"

The old man ran a comb through his hair in preparation for the evening meal. "Lord, the memorabilia on my walls bring two thoughts to mind, even though supper time beckons: my mind praises You, and I yearn for reunion with my Katy."

THE MENTOR AND THE MENTOREE

A light rain passed over the Center through the night. The sky cleared by mid-morning. Cardinals sang with joy. The early morning cutting of grass by groundskeepers left a faint alfalfa smell while Brother Shad and his young pastor friend, Chris, walked side by side, absorbed in their theological discussion cut short from the previous afternoon.

"This time of year entices me to make time for short walks through the majestic trees and around the colorful flowers on your campus," Chris asserted. He bent down to cradle a blossom in his hand, careful not to break its stem. Four turkeys meandered around the lawn by the office complex as the two men completed the elder pastor's first one-mile circuit at the Center.

Brother Shad hesitated, "Your theological conclusions ring true, but you need more depth in your explanations." Then with aggression in his eyes, he reached down to pluck out three new dandelion shoots. A look of satisfaction crossed his face, "into the dumpster with you."

He slapped his hands together several times, as an expression of satisfaction spread across his face. With clean fingers, he smirked: "You other yellow-crowned stems, don't make the same mistake. When I come by tomorrow, don't grow, or I shall pull you out of the ground."

The two pastors continued an animated discussion with an analysis of Brother Shad's sermon outline for the word *great.* The points of the outline generated questions in the mind of the young preacher about Christ's atoning sacrifice traced through the Book of Hebrews.

Brother Shad answered each question with either a "yes" or "no," and then explained his responses. He smiled at his mild-mannered young friend, "Shall we call this barrage of interrogation questions a final seminary exam? I like your insatiable hunger for Bible knowledge." Chris' inquisitive mind, like a sponge, soaked up every drop of advice the veteran Bible expositor uttered.

Their walk completed and now back inside the building, his stocky friend pressed an inquiry, "Brother Shad, when did you last preach John 14:6? You know, the passage in which Jesus said: 'I am the way, the truth and the life?'"

Shad hesitated in the doorway to his room, "I remember I first preached that verse at age seventeen. My older sister forced me to substitute for her one night at a revival meeting conducted in a town fifty miles away from our home."

He stroked his chin and recounted the event. "She left the revival and returned to our home on the train. But before the train departed, she instructed me to stay, play the guitar, sing with gusto, and preach from my heart. God amazed me. He met needs of individuals in every one those services."

Brother Shad confided to his colleague as they stepped into his room, "My mind does not function well. I can't trust my memory anymore. It fails me. I try to write a letter or prepare a note to send to a friend, after I read my Bible and pray each morning. But my memory escapes me. My problem—five minutes later, I can't remember the person's name."

The young pastor turned to leave and exclaimed: "Maybe so, but your biblical insights bless me. Bye, Brother Shad, I shall come again in a couple of days."

Shad waved good-bye to his eager student and turned to see a visitor seated across the room. Shocked, then pleased, he heard an animated voice sounding forth from the cheerful lady who sat in his lounge chair, "Hi Dad! How's Mister Shadrach today? Let's go to my home for dinner."

A HOME-COOKED MEAL
WEDNESDAY, JUNE 27, 5:00 P.M.

The aroma tantalized both Brother Shad and Tammy when they entered her front door. "I smell a banquet in preparation," the old man said as he sniffed the air. He patted his stomach and headed toward the kitchen. The pot roast simmered, its contents ready for consumption. The smell of vegetables with added spices in the crock pot wafted throughout the house.

He smiled and knew his daughter had mastered the art of cooking long before her mother passed on to join Jesus. He knew from previous get-togethers he would never experience a bad meal in her home. Dinner at his daughter's table, ever delightful, once again evolved into a feast.

"Dad, I will serve dinner in 30 minutes. Come, sit down at the kitchen table and talk with me while I finish the tossed salad and banana bread."

"Okay. Make it good. I want to savor every bite. My false teeth say click-clack and my mouth waters in anticipation of this special meal."

"I set the table before I came to pick you up. And I placed the glasses beside the red cloth napkins to add to the 4th of July theme on the placemats. Our garden provided the small bouquet of rose blossoms to decorate the table. Mom gave me the white tablecloth with gold trim border on my 40th birthday. I thought you would enjoy the table setting today. Remember Dad, Grandpa and Grandma Milburn gave this table cloth to you and Mom at your wedding?"

"I remember the day. Your Mother thought it the best gift she had ever received."

Tammy gave him no time for further reflection. "Melody arrives in about ten minutes. She helps coordinate details at church for the young people involved in a senior-high mime drama which they will present next week at our 4th of July service."

"Will she take a leading role in the cast?"

"No. However, she does perform a small role, but accepted a bigger responsibility in the preparation of costumes, a huge undertaking for a senior."

"I pray the production goes well," he responded, swallowing a drink of water, "and that it glorifies Jesus."

"Dad, I believe this team will perform in a manner that will make all of us happy."

Tammy paused in her preparation of the banana bread, a look of concern on her face. "Melody shows industriousness in all her activities. She works hard to develop her talents.

"You haven't seen her for six weeks. I see new maturity. She plans ahead for each day of her summer school schedule." With pride in her voice, she added, "This young lady makes me feel proud of her accomplishments."

"Now, I look forward to TWO super events today: your fine dinner and a visit with my granddaughter Melody."

They heard steps on the front porch. Brother Shad looked toward the living room and acknowledged, "Here she comes."

Bear, the Huskie, barked as Melody walked in quick steps across the front porch. The clock chimed 5:15 p.m. Even the two goldfish in the glass bowl set in a corner of the kitchen responded by fast darts and dives in their small water tank. Both animals and fish knew life with impetuous Melody was never dull.

Dropping her school backpack in the living room, she greeted the occupants in the kitchen, kicking her shoes to the side of the stairs. "Hi, Grandpa! Hi, Mom! Boy, what a great rehearsal today at the church. Say Mom, what's for dinner?" My nose wants my hungry body to sit down at the table right now!"

"Pot roast smothered with veggies, salad, and banana bread. Give Grandpa a hug and a kiss, then wash for dinner. We can sit down at the table in five minutes."

"Okay, Mom. But first, let me tell you, Kevin did a fantastic job in rehearsal today as George Washington." Melody talked with hands moving everywhere and with her body in constant motion emphasizing her strong convictions. "Our mime presentation will be fabulous. He gained coordination and conviction in his actions and movements this week.

"Grandpa, Kevin, a boy in my class, lives three doors west, around the corner on Yellow Pine Street. Skeptical at first, he tried out for a part. I talked him into the audition. His creative and artistic ability show; he proved himself capable of the lead."

Impetuous Melody turned around and quickly found a place to sit on her Grandpa's lap. He enjoyed the attention, but sputtered: "You will ruin the press line in my pants if you continued to squirm. Also, this chair might break like kindling wood under the additional weight, with both of us crashing to the floor."

With her quick wit, she gave her Grandpa a hug and two quick, peck-like kisses on his left cheek in response. Jumping up, she bent over, stuck her face close to his ear, and exclaimed, "Grandpa, I love you! I look forward to dinner with you this evening." With that burst of enthusiasm, she picked up her backpack and shoes and ran up the stairs to wash for dinner.

In a few minutes, the three generations sat at the dining room table with the food dishes placed between Tammy and her dad for ease of serving. She smiled at her two loved ones, took a deep breath, and looked at her Dad: "Will you ask the Lord's blessing on our meal together tonight?"

"My pleasure, sweetie. 'Precious Heavenly Father, we come to You in the magnificent name of Jesus. We give thanks for this bountiful meal You placed before us. Bless it to our bodies as we partake of this delicious dinner and help us remember all good things come from You, Lord, our Provider, Helper, and the One who takes care of our every need. For this, we give You all glory, honor, and praise. In Jesus' great and powerful name we pray. Amen.'"

"Dad, will you serve the pot roast to each of us, please? Careful, the bowl is hot. It retains heat for a long time."

"Okay, my dear! I shall enjoy the honor." He ladled the portions, careful that nothing spilled on to the aged tablecloth.

"Hurry up, Grandpa. I'm hungry!" Grandpa Shad served the pot roast and veggies while Melody continued a report about her school activities and church involvement. Grandpa Shad and her mother had little chance to respond throughout much of the meal. Their part of the conversation acknowledged Melody's enthusiasm with short statements like: "Ooh" or "Yes" or "I see" or "Interesting" or "Amazing" or "Um hum" or some other short expletive uttered between enjoyable mouthfuls of Tammy's scrumptious dinner.

Melody the fussbudget, jumped up after the meal and cleared the table of dishes. She managed to help her mother each day with a minimum of clean-up activities. Then she quickly excused herself to go to her room to complete school assignments. She practiced her mime for the 4th of July drama, and played through her oboe music for the school band.

"Dad, it seems two projects demand Melody's immediate attention at the same time every day after school, whether at school, at church, or at home with me. I think life with Melody, not a circus, nor slow-paced, but eventful and a hardy stimulation for my arteries."

Tammy incurred no problems with sleepless nights. But prayers for her high-spirited daughter challenged her stamina and ingenuity.

Tonight, Melody followed her usual routine. She conversed with her Grandpa for a few minutes, then excused herself and headed to her room for study. Tammy sighed, "I'll clean up the rest of the kitchen. Then we can relax in the living room and I'll tell you more of Melody's fast-track lifestyle."

Grandpa Shad shared a few devotional thoughts with Tammy to ease her anxiety while she finished the kitchen clean-up. As they walked to the living room, Shad tried to address Melody's hyperactivity. "'What mighty works and deeds of power are performed by the Lord's hands' (Mark 6:2). We rest in His hands, the hands of our Creator who reaches out to us with His love.

"The hands of our Lord shaped the universe by His deeds of power, cleansed the lepers, broke the chains of sin, healed the blind, and raised the dead." Tammy wasn't convinced, but let her dad speak without interruption. "The One who shaped the universe hears our every cry. He looks after us in every situation."

In the living room, Brother Shad reached for his daughter's hands. "He holds our hands; we don't hold His. We sit inscribed 'on the palms of' His hands (Isaiah 49:16). Let us remember, God does not forget you, Melody, or me. His hands around ours keep us safe in all situations. Tammy, God hears our prayers. By these scriptures He promised to protect us. Let us continue our prayer for Melody. God indeed, works out our concerns." Just the sound of her dad's voice gave her comfort.

"Let us continue to bind the enemy—that Liar. Right now, let's pray for the power of the blood of Jesus to cover Melody, and for the Holy Spirit to give guidance over her spirit. I know God will give success and good answers to our prayers, because God guides both of you. He works His good pleasure in both of you every day."

"Thank you, Dad, for the encouragement." She admitted to herself, her dad's counsel always gave her relief and support. "Why don't you say good-bye to Melody? Then I'll drive you back to the Center, because I must prepare for my Library conference tomorrow."

Moving slowly, Grandpa Shad walked to the stairs, raised his tired voice. He spoke with hesitation: "Melody, Grandpa here. I must return, to my home. Come down, please. . . . Give me one more hug, and a kiss good-bye."

Melody ran down the stairs and spoke with enthusiasm. "Oh, Grandpa, please come again soon. I miss you! And don't forget about our 4th of July Sunday evening mime drama. It will thrill your heart. I have an important part.

Parting with Grandpa Shad brought tears to Melody's eyes. These close buddies, two generations apart, shared a special relationship, a bond of love and respect that spanned the 76 years between them.

Melody wondered: *How many more dinners might we share before Jesus calls Grandpa Home?* To her, Grandpa Shad had a solid answer to every problem she encountered. "Grandpa, I love your humor and your ability to make a person feel important."

Tammy and her Dad walked with care down the steps to her car. Brother Shad paused for a moment, looked up at the stars in the Milky Way, while Tammy unlocked and opened the door for him on the passenger side. In that moment he gazed skyward, again the question surfaced in his mind: "How long, Lord? I'm ready, Jesus. Will it be tonight?"

CHAPTER FIVE

SUCCESSFUL BIBLE BITS

*Your word I have hidden in my heart,
that I might not sin against You.*
Psalm 119:11

JONAH'S PRAYER AND EXPRESSION OF FAITH
WEDNESDAY, JULY 11, 6:30 P.M.

BUSY SCHEDULES FOR TAMMY and Melody often necessitated the postponement of scheduled dinners with Brother Shad. Today, however, Tammy excelled with her dad's favorite grilled chicken with amber rice casserole dinner. Afterward, the three sat around the kitchen table involved in family chit-chat, dessert in hand.

"I want to make this dish of mint chocolate-chip ice cream last as long as possible," Brother Shad exclaimed. "Even this raisin cookie on my plate," he smiled, "I shall consume bit by bit. I will not exercise any rush to end this memorable event." The ice cream brought out his good humor. Happiness prevailed.

One of Melody's questions elicited a long response from her Grandpa when she asked, "Grandpa, as an international evangelist, what happened when you preached in the Philippines?"

Tammy had not heard all the facts of this trip. She leaned her elbows on the table, "Tell us, Dad, about your ministry in that part of Asia Pacific." Her inquisitiveness raised the question, "Which one of your topics brought the most souls into the kingdom?"

"I think I can best answer your question by relating my success with Jonah. I remember at age 45, I preached about Jonah for a pastor's meeting at a Bible school in Southern Mindanao. My morning chapel message emphasized truth. Thus, I began: Jonah learned that one person used of God could turn a wicked nation to the Lord."

Melody rolled her eyes. *I've heard this story before.*

The sermon, hidden in the recesses of his mind, poured out in torrents. Brother Shad spoke with conviction: "Jonah felt it unthinkable to leave King Jeroboam II (793-753 B.C.) of Israel. Why? Because, he felt the king needed him. Thus, if he left Israel, he would not show patriotism to his country."

Melody feared a lecture about to block the joy of savoring her ice cream.

"Read the text and you can feel Jonah's lament: 'Lord, did you not appoint my voice for Israel?' Jonah's prestige turned to pride. He affirmed, 'A man of my position should not give utterances of condemnation.'"

Melody ate silently, feeling she had asked her Grandpa the wrong question.

"Vanity filled Jonah's mind, even though the call from God sounded clear in his conscience. God instructed: 'Go to Nineveh! Preach against that city. Cry out against their wickedness!' (Jonah 1:2; 3:2). Instead, Jonah ran away from God's call on his life. A command like this from the Lord left Jonah dumbfounded. 'I'm confused,' he replied, 'my faith shaken.'"

"Oh, Grandpa, every first grader knows the story of Jonah. Why did you preach a kiddies' story that morning?"

"Perhaps, Melody, we may hear new insights from the Book of Jonah. Let's listen," Tammy admonished Melody, and then smiled to encourage her Dad.

"The Lord always instructed me by His Holy Spirit what I needed to preach. The Lord gave me specific orders wherever he sent me." Shad's hand pointed to some faraway land out the window, "just like he did with Jonah.

"That prophet refused at first to reach out to others with the Word of God. Those Mindanao pastors to whom I preached, failed to reach out with the Word to people in their own communities."

"OK. Tell me more, Grandpa." Melody stood up to take her dishes to the kitchen sink. "I want to hear your version of Jonah."

"I want to hear these spiritual truths, too," Tammy affirmed as she rinsed their plates and saucers and loaded each piece into her dishwasher.

"Jonah determined to run away in the opposite direction. He wanted to escape from any connection with the Ninevites. He heard they tore off the hands and lips of their victims." Shad leaned forward and made chopping hand motions. "They were cruel oppressors.

"The challenge appeared too great for him. He ran away from God's call and boarded a ship bound for Spain." Brother Shad's hands illustrated each facet of his explanations. He could not talk without using his hands.

"You know the story, Melody," his gaze pierced her inquisitiveness. "The ship ran into a gigantic typhoon that swirled around them. The storm grew wilder and more violent by the minute. When the men on the ship found out he had run away from God, he told the sailors to throw him overboard in order to save themselves.

"At first, the terrified crew refused, but at last consented to his request. Thrown overboard, his body seemed bound by chains. Yet, by the sailor's actions, the storm immediately ceased, the sea turned glassy smooth and still." Shad's body movements imitated those of Jonah. His actions frozen in time.

Both women looked at each other, then at Shad, wondering *What will he do next to illustrate his version of this 'fish' story?*

"But, poor Jonah. He didn't have time to change into a swimsuit, much less pack a suitcase for his underwater journey. The Lord, however, sent a large fish—big like a freight truck, to pick up Jonah. Oh course, he stepped in. I imagine you would call it the late night run of the Joppa to Rome Fish-mobile Express."

"Oh, Grandpa!" Melody felt embarrassed. "How you exaggerate."

"Dad, did you preach in this exaggerated way to the Filipinos?" Tammy spoke up, eyebrows raised, registering unbelief.

Brother Shad ignored their skepticism and continued the narrative with his next breath, "Jonah ran away from God, first on foot, next in a freight ship, now in a fish-mobile. But the Lord in His mercy made a water bed for Jonah to sleep on throughout those three days and nights inside the fish. No one objected to his snoring. He could enjoy his own private swimming pool. But for some reason, no lights would turn on in this underwater hotel.

"I think he experienced a blackout. He, of course, went to the banqueting table by himself, a delicious menu of seaweed salad and broken coconut branches. He did not cook anything; meal service offered raw delicacies that stunk. You wouldn't call it a vacation. He had no radio, no TV, no newspaper, no cell phone, not even a friend to keep him company or with whom to share this underwater journey."

"Grandpa, what an imagination! Did you always dramatize your stories and sermons like this one?" Melody began to realize her Grandpa had the ability to tell a good story.

"I like your story-telling, Dad. Sounds exciting," Tammy laughed.

"No, Melody, not to this extent," Shad interjected. "But notice, God placed Jonah in a slimy, underwater jail. No offshore breezes cooled him off at night and he found no fresh water for bathing in the daytime. No one gave him a key to the front door of that jail cell, but God. And that key was prayer."

"Now I understand, Grandpa. Tell me more." Melody sensed a spiritual truth forthcoming.

"Jonah knew he must talk to God about the entire situation. Some people, Melody, pray while in bed, others pray when out for a walk on the street. Some kneel, many sit in a chair and pray. The important point to remember: pray wherever you wish, and whenever needed, pray. Jonah prayed way down deep inside a slimy stomach that gurgled and bubbled."

Ice cream and cookie consumed, Brother Shad began to walk about as he told his story, hands on his hips. "In his mountain-moving prayer of chapter two, Jonah quoted parts of several psalms. In the process, he repented, rededicated his life to the Lord, and answered the call God placed on his life.

"Notice Jonah's confession: 'I called out of my distress to the Lord, and He answered me' (Jonah 2:2). The phrase comes from Psalm 18:6. Thereafter this shamed prophet acknowledged, 'With the voice of thanksgiving, that which I vowed I will make good, I will do it' (Jonah 2:9). This passage comes from Psalm 50:14."

Melody and Tammy listened carefully to every word. They could feel the growing tension in the elder Milburn's description of the drowning prophet's grasp for life.

"I see real depth of character behind Jonah's fear of the Ninevites," Tammy interjected. "But he walked with God in a disjointed manner, although in an awesome relationship."

Shad smiled, lowered his voice, and kept his concentration intact. "Jonah had committed much of God's Word to memory in his earlier life. Similarly, we also need to memorize God's Word. It gives us a direct line to heaven. You can hear Jonah shout in the belly of the fish: 'I will go, Lord! I will go! I will do what you want me to do!'

"To Jonah's amazement, the Lord answered his request and rededication by commanding the fish to vomit up Jonah and cast him out on the sea shore." The heightened drama caused Melody's stomach muscles to cramp.

"Can you imagine the scene of Jonah's expulsion from the fish?"

Blaaah!

"The fish, possibly two freight trucks wide, probably spit him high in the air. I think if seaweed had not been entangled around his neck, Jonah might have seen Rome to the left and Jerusalem to the right.

"Thereafter, when he hit the ground, I believe he ran toward Nineveh. He would not have turned around, nor even taken time to thank the fish for the deliverance. He did not even telephone his mom to tell her he was okay, because he found no available cell phone service in that area."

"Dad, your imagery has gone too far out for me," Tammy blushed and covered her face with her hands.

"Grandpa," Melody's tension abated. "I can't believe your imagination. Did you take a creative writing course in high school or college?"

"No. But *you* might consider it. It will help you organize your thoughts and communication skills." Shad knew he had to deliver a convincing conclusion. "Jonah's deliverance from the fish shows that God allows men to cooperate with Him.

"This story tells us that God holds His servants accountable and responsible to himself. The spiritual truth for us to remember: those who know God should tell those who do not know God. God's people serve as channels for God's blessings to other people."

"You made a strong case for servant-hood, Dad. I think the Lord blessed your Philippines trip with many souls, too."

"And, we know, Grandpa," Melody added, "Jonah preached with tremendous success in Nineveh. Our Sunday school teacher made that fact clear to us last year."

FEDERICO AND THE SWORDFISH

Shad sat down, quieted himself, gave Melody a loving grandfather hug, and said, "I want to relate a parallel incident, a true story, which transpired the same year I went to the Southern Philippines. A pastor there recounted this incident to me. He told me a young fisherman by the name of Federico, who lived nearby in Southern Mindanao, didn't learn these same lessons soon enough in his life.

"Federico went out to fish one night in May per his custom. By 11:30 p.m., he found his regular fishing spot in the big bay. Suddenly, like a cannon shot, an eight-foot-long swordfish jumped out of the water and on its downward turn, stabbed him in the right side as he sat in his long, narrow, boat. The first miracle of this story—the swordfish did not flip him into the sea when it fell back into the water."

"Oh Grandpa, my heart started to beat fast, again. I think," she placed her hand on her chest, "it even skipped a beat."

"Federico lost consciousness in about 20 minutes. Fortunately, a nearby fisherman towed him back to shore and within an hour, took him to the hospital. Four people, including his mother and the two lady co-pastors of the local church he attended, entered into intense prayer and felt impressed by the Holy Spirit that he would recover.

"They believe the reason this freak accident occurred was that he had promised his mother three weeks earlier that, henceforth, he would live a Christian life. At the time, she suffered with pneumonia in the local hospital. Her prayer: 'Lord, before You take me home, I want to see all of my children serve You.'"

Tammy, caught up in the excitement of the story, whistled, and remarked, "God wanted that man to serve Him."

"Federico made a commitment earlier in his life to follow God. But after one week, he set his resolve aside and continued his old lifestyle of drinking and gambling. Then, God intervened in an unexpected way.

"None of the fishermen in the little coast-line village had ever heard of this type of accident. They ask each other, 'Of all the space in the open sea, why would a swordfish choose to surface at that particular spot, come down, and stab a person in his boat?'"

"I think," Melody reasoned, "God wanted his tithe or maybe his willingness to preach."

"Federico rededicated his life to the Lord his first day in the hospital. Then another miracle happened—the hospital sent him home in one week after just one operation. Beforehand, the doctor had estimated his stay in the hospital would last at least two weeks and require two operations.

"The swordfish had cut an '*S*' in his liver which caused internal bleeding. One of the village wives said that '*S*' stood for Satan. But after Federico rededicated his life to the Lord, another wife commented, His 'S' stands for 'Saved.'"

"Grandpa, are you telling me a true story?"

"Yes. Remember, my dear, when God places a call on your life, answer Him right away and respond the first time. Don't delay. Melody, give God's mission for your life first priority. Whatever method or way it may come to you, prepare to go and reach the unreached for Christ, whether here or far away.

"The Book of Jonah excites me because it resembles a window through which God permits us to see His heart's desire. He lets us know we cannot limit our love and sympathy for some of our fellow human beings or exclude it from others. God didn't give Jonah an option. He needed to obey, and in a similar manner, we each must obey His call on our own life. You see, God encourages us at all times: 'Go out and reach the unreached for Christ.'"

"Dad, I like your story-telling and spiritual principles, even right here in my kitchen."

Settled into bed that night, Melody remained awake longer than usual, and reflected upon the spiritual truths she had learned from the life of Jonah. Grandpa Shad's observations deserved serious consideration. He, indeed, had experienced the fire of life's rough experiences. He knew people; he knew what the Lord desired; he knew the way of truth and righteousness.

Melody determined before she fell asleep, "I must never forget these lessons, Grandpa."

She spoke out loud as if he stood beside her in the darkened room. "I shall do my best to make these truths a part of my life."

THE PLAID SHIRTS
THURSDAY, JULY 19, 9:00 A.M.

"Let me see," Brother Shad looked into his mirror. "I shaved and put on clean underwear this morning. I think I'll wear the same socks I wore yesterday. Hmm, I could have worn these socks Tuesday. They don't appear stiff. Anyway, I like these colors of red and blue. This shirt doesn't look bad. I like it. Oh, oh! The seam on these pants pulled out by the pocket. Well, I've got them on now. I'll just wear them for today. Too much bother to change."

Brother Shad talked out loud to himself while he dressed. It helped him focus his thoughts. This monologue occurred every day in his morning preparation time. He finished his ritual, then heard the sharp rhythmical sound of high-heeled shoes on the tiled floor outside his doorway—click-clomp, click-clomp. He smiled. "Aah, Matti will soon appear."

"Hi, Brother Shad."

"Good day to you, too, Matti. Please come and sit down by me."

"What thought came to you this morning from the Good Book?"

"I read the Book of Revelation. Chapter one, verse three says: 'Blessed is he who reads and those who hear the words of this prophecy.' Matti, we meet Jesus on page after page of this final book of the Bible. The Book of Revelation gives us hope—hope for now, hope for tomorrow, hope for our future. Jesus, the Victorious One wins the last battle. He assures our salvation."

"Hallelujah," Matti raised her hands in praise. "God's hope applies to every situation in our life, does it not?"

"Yes, Matti. Jesus remains forever faithful. In all of my 94 years and four months, He has never failed me." Brother Shad spoke with decisiveness, his eyes sparkled.

"Me neither, for my 82 years and five months," Matti agreed, catching his positive outlook for the day.

This type of dialogue each day between the two friends often proceeded in a formal, yet spirited and friendly manner. Brother Shad enjoyed Matti's company because he felt few people ever came to visit. Matti came almost every other day to check on him, encourage him, and assess his physical condition and mental acuity.

On the days she didn't visit, she telephoned, "Matti here, Brother Shad." She considered Brother Shad part of her family. Their warm friendship exuded a concerned brother-sister relationship. Often, her first question to him: "What did they serve you for breakfast this morning?"

His daughter Tammy had brought Brother Shad to the Center after his wife Katy died. In years since then, he and Matti had discussed a relationship agreement, because the transition period in the lives of both seniors exhibited grief for lost mates. The life of his deceased Katy and confidante crept into each conversation.

Matti still grieved for her deceased husband Dan several years after his death. In these sunset years, Brother Shad would pour out his love for his deceased Katy, for his daughter Tammy, even for Matti.

"I know you love me, Brother Shad," she spoke slowly and firmly. "But we share a brother-sister kind of love."

"Yes, Matti," he sighed. "I know you're right."

"And I love you, Brother Shad, not only like a brother, but as a true friend." Her voice raised in pitch and volume. "The Lord made our special relationship possible at this time for the benefit of both of us."

"I do understand." He tearfully looked out the window for a moment, then attested, "I appreciate your frankness and care for me. It seems you come with a sharper eye for my welfare than the nurses and attendants out around the corner. They try their best, of course, to serve and comfort people. But God bless you, Matti," he smiled, "for your kindness to me."

With initial pleasantries exchanged, Aunt Matti's eyes gave Brother Shad's shirt a critical examination. "Your shirt needs another wash job, my friend. I see food stains in three places by your buttons."

"It's okay, Matti. I do not plan to go anywhere today, except to the dining room."

"Brother Shad, my reason for this visit today: I want to give you these two new shirts—one long-sleeved and one short-sleeved. Your shirts look thin from constant wear."

"You fuss over me too much, Matti. I'm embarrassed." He held up one shirt, then the other. "Where did you find these shirts? Oh, they look nice. I will enjoy wearing the blue and grey plaid and I like this cowboy shirt style. Look at those quick-snap buttons. I think that's the best kind for me. Reminds me of my teenage days in Canada. Give a quick yank and—all unbuttoned. Easy on, easy off."

"Go into your bathroom and change into the one you like best, please. Then, give me your food-stained shirt," she commanded. "We shall place it in your dirty clothes bag."

"Oh, Matti," he pleaded. "I just finished dressing a few minutes ago. You're talking to me like my wife, Katy. She ran a good household operation."

"I know," she spoke with encouragement and in softer tones. "However, I want to see how you look in this beautiful plaid shirt. You said you have no place to go. Please take time to change. I shall wait for you to make the switch before I go visit elsewhere."

"Matti, you remind me of Katy, my dear lady who knew how to take care of me and my clothes. Okay," he chuckled. "Please excuse me for a couple of minutes. . . ."

"The shirt fits you well my friend," she stood up, looked him over, and pulled at the material on his shoulder with approval. "It makes you look quite handsome." Matti knew his sizes and preferences. She had grown up with three brothers and had learned men's habits and ways of living. With this comment, she excused herself and said: "I want to visit three other people in the Center this morning before lunchtime."

Brother Shad smiled, waved good-bye as she left his room, and thought: *"That Matti, of all my friends, she knows how to look after me and dote on me in a most persistent, yet encouraging way."*

VISITORS A-PLENTY

He turned, walked toward the window, settled down into his dilapidated chair and read the first eight verses of chapter one in the Book of Revelation. At that moment, his second visitor of the day, the stern-faced Nurse Hotchkiss appeared in his doorway and interrupted his devotional time.

"Mister Milburn, I did not take your blood pressure and pulse yesterday. Please roll up your shirt sleeve."

"I shall comply with a smile. I feel good today. A friend stopped by earlier and gave me this new shirt. I like it. Do you?"

"Yes, a nice plaid. It makes you look dignified," she observed in a detached manner, her attention focused on the blood pressure gauge. "You seem excited, I think, from your friend's visit. Blood pressure: 168 over 95."

"Continue your medicine. I don't want any problems with you." This time, when Nurse Hotchkiss spoke, a slight smile creased the corner of her mouth. She admired Brother Shad for his tenacity in Bible study and for his knowledge of Bible prophecy.

On her previous round last Tuesday, she confided to Brother Shad she had given her life to the Lord only nine months earlier. "What were you reading as I entered your room, Mister Milburn?"

"My mind focused on Revelation 1:8. Jesus confirms He is the 'Alpha and the Omega, the Beginning and the End, who is and who was and who is to come, the Almighty.' This passage shows Jesus as prophet, priest, judge, and king. Chapter one, therefore, encourages and excites me. This part of the Bible informs us of the tremendous scope of Jesus' ministry."

"Agreed. Those thoughts give me hope. Nevertheless, I repeat Mr. Milburn, continue your medicine regimen." With that declaration and only a hint of being sociable, Nurse Hotchkiss exited the room, head erect, shoulders back, the business-as-usual expression again written on her face.

"Who will bless me next with their presence?" Brother Shad chuckled as he spoke out loud to himself. "Can I call it my day for visitors? Most days, my only guests, not actual guests, number the morning breakfast server and the shift duty nurse: 'Hello -- take this pill -- good-bye.' For what reason, I wonder, do I warrant popularity today?"

Time did not allow further speculation about the human traffic jam in his room. Gregory, a cleaning attendant, appeared in his doorway moments after Nurse Hotchkiss exited. Gregory knocked politely on the door to attract Brother Shad's attention: "Mister Shad, sir, housekeeping sent me to dust your room and mop the floor."

"Come right in, young man." Brother Shad waved his hand and noticed the deep bronze tone of Gregory's complexion. "Tell me, where were you born?"

"Jamaica, sir. Then I attended Tuskegee Tech for two years."

"How did you arrange to be employed by the Center?"

"My brother lives in town. I needed a job in order to go back and complete my social work studies at Tuskegee Tech." Gregory had begun dusting and setting small items in order as he spoke. "I stay with him, work here to save money, and pay my next year school bills."

"May the Lord bless and help you, Gregory. While you clean my room, I shall go down to the activities room around the corner. Please come and tell me when you finish."

Brother Shad left his room and wondered, *who will I talk to next on my day for visitors?*

Turning the corner at the end of the corridor, near the activities room, Brother Shad stopped his measured, feeble walk and expressed wonderment at the middle-aged couple who walked toward him. *They look familiar.*

"Brother Shad, we came to see you today. How are you, dear pastor friend?"

"Hello to you both. You bring back recollections of church board meetings we shared several years ago."

"Yes, good recall. Fifteen years ago in Omaha, you and Katy, the four of us, went out for dinner after our convention."

He held the hand of each person, looked from one to the other, and said: "Tell me your names, please. I remember your faces, but my memory fails me."

"Sid and Sandra Ridenhorst, we saw you almost three months ago at Dolly's Ice Cream Parlor and ten years earlier in the Lincoln Mall."

"I remember. You purchased clothes for one of your college boys. Katy and I shopped in Lincoln that day for a new suit for me.

We crossed paths, an unplanned meeting that Friday morning at the center of the Mall. Katy and I stood beside a jewelry store."

"Correct. Mary, the wife of our first son, the doctor, delivered another boy. Our number two son, the electrical engineer, stays busy raising two girls."

The reconnection conversation continued for twenty minutes at a table near a window in a corner of the activities room. The delightful reunion with his old friends raised Brother Shad's spirits, interrupted only by the bell for lunch as it sounded over the public-address system.

Sid and Sandra excused themselves and expressed to Brother Shad their joy in the visit with him. "We promise to come again after the completion of arrangements for our second son who will enroll in graduate school." After good-byes with warm embraces, each party turned, walked away, lost in their own thoughts.

Brother Shad ambled down the corridor past his room and looked for his three dining room partners, He walked with a swagger on his two stiff legs toward the dining room. The four men always sat together at a table by the window in the southwest corner. At the dining room doorway, Max, one of his table partners, entered with the other two, Phillip with Henry, close behind. "Max," Brother Shad chuckled, "this morning I received more visitors than cheers given for a freshman boy who threw the winning point in a basketball tournament."

"Let's hear the good news, Brother Shad," responded Max. "Give us the details." The dining room ritual had started seven years earlier when Brother Shad first arrived at the City Center. Each of the other men had come at different times within the last five years, each one at different times a ministerial co-worker with Brother Shad.

Max, an evangelist for thirty years, first met Brother Shad when both preached a seniors camp meeting at the Heartstone Campground in South Dakota.

"Did you preach many sermons at the Campground?" Phillip questioned. "If you did, I'm hurt you didn't tell me ahead of time that I might have called out the choir." Phillip directed a church music program and choir in Oregon for many years. He and Brother Shad met at a regional church prayer conference when Brother Shad was the speaker and Phillip directed the choir of delegates and members of neighboring churches.

Henry, a retired layman from Ohio, said: "I could ask housekeeping to bake a cake and serve coffee and punch with a couple of peanuts thrown in. I feel lunch today deserves a journal event for my diary." He and his wife hosted Brother Shad and his wife Katy whenever scheduled into his home church. Their fellowship over the years grew into a family relationship. The men became like brothers, the women wrote letters to each other like sisters.

What did these men talk about each noon in the dining room? Their wives and children. The bond between the four had strengthened over the weeks and months since last Thanksgiving. The lives of each man's children were shared among the dinner partners. Recent good news from the children of one man encouraged the other men for the welfare of their own children.

"Send your visitors my way," Max requested, one eye partially closed. "Live companionship beats irritable and miserable TV programs."

"Yes," replied Brother Shad. However, his mind dwelt non-stop on the Word of God undistracted by popular culture. But with the progression of his dementia each month, he concentrated less on prayer for the family affairs of the other men.

After the noon meal, he arose slowly from their table and declared, "Gentlemen, please excuse me for my nap time. Perhaps Jesus might come for me this afternoon. I often wonder, who will I see, and who I will not see in heaven?"

CHAPTER SIX

SUMMER DEATH UNEXPECTED
Our citizenship is in heaven.
Philippians 3:20

A DINNER PARTNER GONE HOME
THURSDAY, JULY 19, 7:00 P.M.

TALL, THIN HENRY KNOCKED on Brother Shad's door and spoke in labored bursts: "Our dinner buddy, Max, the evangelist . . . went to the Lord (sob) . . . after supper, this evening!"

"Why not me, Lord?" Brother Shad exclaimed with an audible groan, both hands placed on his forehead.

"He sat down," Henry moaned, "in his chair . . . he just went to sleep. The evening nurse found Him, slumped over (snort) . . . as she began, her evening round (cough) . . . of passing out medication."

"The kindness of Jesus made possible his departure without trauma," Brother Shad said with a fixed gaze at Henry's tear-filled eyes. "I hope the Lord will take me the same way."

"Now (sigh) . . . we will see an empty chair, at our table." Overcome with grief, Henry continued to cry.

"Console yourself, Henry. 'To be absent from the body' is 'to be present with the Lord' (2 Corinthians 5:8). Our Lord will not forsake us. Max's death saddens me, too. But even with one less person at our dinner table, I feel happy for him to dwell in his new residence, where 'there shall be no more death nor sorrow . . . nor crying' nor pain (Revelation 21:4)."

"Death, funerals, caskets, ambulances, mortuaries—it all distresses me," Henry agonized with his hands on his face. "God proved merciful to Max," his weeping continued. "He will receive many rewards (gasp), for hundreds of souls (wheeze), he brought into the Kingdom."

Brother Shad sought to console Henry. But the opposite response erupted. Henry's shoulders shook. His face turned ashen. His eyes continued to tear. Out of Henry's innermost bowls spewed disjointed feelings of despair, "Oh, what shall we do?" Distraught, Henry became incoherent, "I . . . we, he . . . ."

"Henry, come, sit down. Give me your hand." Brother Shad pulled the straight-back chair over near his lounge chair for Henry.

"Why did it happen? What will we do without Max? I don't feel well. I think I have a headache. I came to tell you (groan), as soon as I heard the news. Who will go next? Is this Center just a waiting place for the death of us all? A corral, a holding pen for the coroner's next visit?

"Shad, my heart skips beats. I feel hot in my face. My heart wants to explode in my chest. Please call the nurse to take me to my room. I need a wheelchair." He continued to gasp for air and speculated: "Will the Lord call me next?"

"Henry, Henry, Henry. I don't believe today marks your day. Take slow, deep breaths. While you do that, I'll call the nurse. She will bring a wheelchair. Sit still a few moments and consider God's magnificent grace and complete peace. I, too, feel saddened, but happy for Max to see the Lord, yet mystified because he showed no signs of illness earlier at supper."

The night nurse arrived in moments, gave Henry a sedative, and wheeled him to his room. Brother Shad found no time to react to Max's demise until Henry's departure because of his concern for Henry's welfare. He prayed, "Lord, may my departure progress in peace like Max's home-going."

The clock on his dresser indicated: time to turn on the TV for the Thursday night Billy Graham program. Shad watched little TV because it interfered with his Bible study. "When I watch a Christian program," he told Nurse Hotchkiss on one of her recent evening rounds, "I must remember to close my door. I don't want the high volume to disturb my neighbors."

Tonight, he enjoyed a Billy Graham rerun, a review of the 1974 Rio de Janeiro Crusade. Cliff Barrows conducted the preliminary events, and George Beverly Shea sang with excellence, which encouraged Shad to sing with them. Then, Reverend Graham began his talk to the tens of thousands of people assembled. The program lifted Brother Shad's spirit from the depressed state he experienced with his overwrought dinner partner, Henry, and the demise of their friend Max.

Brother Shad felt a part of the program as the Holy Spirit anointed Billy Graham's message. Hundreds of persons came forward to dedicate their lives to Jesus. Brother Shad went to bed that evening, contented and relaxed with snatches of "Just as I Am" on his lips as he turned off the lights and pulled the blanket up to his chin.

While still awake, he turned to his left side and took a deep breath. He set aside the heartache of the day and prayed, "Jesus, take care of and bless my Tammy, young Melody, Matti, and me, all of us here at the Center. Give all of us a fine night's sleep. May we rest well. Place your angels around us, Father; and Jesus, continue Your blood cover of protection over us. Thank You, Lord. Amen." In moments, sleep overcame his stress of Henry's anguish and the troubled news of Max's departure.

MAX'S FUNERAL

At lunch the next day, Brother Shad's nose curled at the sight of the fruit salad: "Hmm, not my choice. This cold gelatin placed around the fruit does not appeal to me. I like salads with ample amounts of spinach, a sliced tomato, all the ingredients possible, and topped with Ranch Dressing."

Henry sat across the table from Brother Shad. "Henry, you look better today. Did you sleep last night?"

"Yes, Brother Shad, and I feel better today. I think my life perspective returned this morning."

Chaplain Sinclair interrupted their conversation and announced from the center of the dining room, "We shall conduct the funeral service for Max in our Chapel on Monday at 10 a.m., three days from today."

Phillip gasped wide-eyed as Chaplain Sinclair left the room. "I wondered why Max didn't show up this noon. What happened to him?"

"Max received his promotion," Henry replied, eyes downcast toward his plate, "that makes me happy. I know the real Max settled for a home in heaven, not a cramped bed in a pine box. I felt shocked it happened last night when we least expected his departure. I don't believe he suffered from any terminal or brittle illness."

"I, too, feel amazed," Shad focused his eyes on Henry, "at his sudden departure, a young 82 years old. Pour yourself a cup of coffee,

Henry, and tell me about your morning activities." Shad touched Henry's arm, "Did you read your Bible and spend time in prayer?"

"I slept until 7:30," Henry professed, "ate my breakfast, cleaned up, read my Bible for half an hour as usual, and prayed a bit. Later," he smiled and sat up straight, "I went to the activities room and watched a Benny Hinn program on TV, a rerun of one of his Philippine meetings a few years ago. Jesus saved and healed many people." Excitement filled his voice. "People left crutches and wheelchairs beside the platform where Benny spoke and ministered in the gifts of the Spirit."

"God answers Benny's consistent and determined prayer life," Phillip interjected as he wiggled his finger to emphasize his comment. "I feel he believes in the truth of Psalm 30:2: 'O LORD, my God, I cried out to you, and You healed me!' Verse five," he emphasized, "follows with those well-known lines: 'Weeping may endure for a night, but joy comes in the morning!'"

"Henry, we have an awesome God of love," Shad confirmed between bites of his cookie. He provided strength for you to face up to the fact of Max's death and his destiny. You received comfort last night for a good night's sleep and for your acknowledgment of this transition in Max's life. It shows God's care and concern for you." Shad opened both his hands toward heaven in praise and suggested, "Let's thank Him for His goodness."

"Right, Brother Shad," Henry agreed, now settled in his own spirit. "I do believe I see God's hand of guidance in this event. We are blessed by God's arranging the minute details of all our lives.

"How kind of the Lord to pick the time after dinner last night for Max's home-going," Phillip added as he pushed his chair away from the table, "and for strengthening our spirits this noon. Even though we shall miss Max, we praise You, Jesus, for taking him to You."

MONDAY, JULY 23, 10:00 A.M.

Janice, the organist-on-call for the Center, played the various lines of *The Old Rugged Cross* with exquisite combinations of low pedal tones and high piccolo reed melodies. The instrument spoke with force, at times with mellow and delicate soft harmonies, altogether a meaningful musical conversation and presentation with spiritual overtones.

The presence of the Holy Spirit permeated the prelude music throughout each progression of senior favorites: *He Lives, Our Great Savior*, and *No One Ever Cared for Me Like Jesus*. Each attendee enjoyed the chance to catch a glimpse of heaven on earth.

Chaplain Sinclair stood in front of the platform and welcomed the congregation. His words of comfort warmed the participants. "I thank you for your attendance as we celebrate Max's home-going." With raised hands, he looked upward, and began the funeral service with prayer. "We gather here today, Lord, to acknowledge Your faithfulness in the life of our brother and friend Maximillian T. Wintlecosta. Your dutiful servant remained obedient to Your call on his life. . . ."

That prayer, much too long, Brother Shad surmised. *We don't need a two-volume biographical speech. A short three-minute summary will suffice.* Few persons attended the service. Only eight people came to say good-bye to Max: Chaplain Sinclair; Brother Shad; Henry; Phillip; Nellie, the day nurse on Max's wing; Sarah, the choir director from the downtown church; Mister Hornby, the Chinese attendant who worked the second shift in Max's area; and Miss Priscella, the assistant director of the City Center Retirement Home.

No family members attended the service. Henry whispered to Brother Shad: "Rumor circulated, one married daughter of unknown address, lives fifteen miles away in the suburb of Cardville." Everyone heard his comment. "No family names appear on his permanent record, not even his wife's name. And, no one could trace the source of the daughter story."

From the other side of Brother Shad, Phillip added in muffled tones, "People talked of a married daughter with two children. Other unconfirmed reports told of a daughter, now divorced. Max never spoke in my presence of children or grandchildren."

Chaplain Sinclair continued to exhort the small group with his preliminary remarks: "Let us bless and praise the Lord at all times. Let us magnify and exalt His name together. Sarah please lead us in the song, *God Will Take Care of You.* Friends, please turn to hymn number 127. We will sing verses one and four."

As the eight faithful ones sang the hymn, Brother Shad's mind drifted to another funeral several years earlier. In his mind, he saw the funeral of his beloved Katy: *Ten years ago -- yes ten years, eleven months, and twenty-nine days. What a difference between Max's funeral and my Katy's celebration. An autumn afternoon, warm and sunny with red, pale green, orange and faded yellow leaves, in free-fall to the ground.* He sighed with heaviness of heart and spoke softly, "I recognized that change of season in my life, because of my Katy's transfer to her heavenly home."

Shad leaned over to Henry's ear and spoke softly with his hand draped in front of his mouth. "As life in the leaves returns to the tree roots in the fall, so my dear Katy relinquished her life. Her soul yielded to the call of her Creator, the root and foundation of her faith."

"My wife," Phillip replied, "died in a train/car accident. She tried to drive across the railroad tracks near a warehouse with a blind corner approach. With no flashing signal light and no traffic barrier arms, the speeding train dragged our car 150 feet down the tracks before it could stop. We could not view her body at the funeral because everything about my lovely wife—crushed."

Brother Shad's mind rolled like a newsreel clip: *The flutter of leaves on the sidewalks and roadways which floated in ripples of capricious motion before their last breath of summer life fell extinguished. Like colored hands which performed a magnificent ballet in the sky, the fall foilage continued, encore after encore throughout the gentle afternoon light breeze.*

Each leaf a part of earth with its life journey completed. Katy's life on earth, now complete, her new life commenced. Brother Shad grieved for her every day. He sighed like one of those dead lifeless leaves. *May my new life begin soon.*

"Gentlemen," Brother Shad uttered, trying not to disrupt the service. "I took care of my beloved for five years as she remained bedridden with osteoporosis and Hodgkin's disease. My friends felt I should have placed her in a nursing home before the end. I couldn't do it, because our relationship had continued for over 57 years."

Their attention returned to Max's service, but Brother Shad's concentration remained stayed on his last days with his wife. *Even though I could not care well for you during those last few months, I tried to comfort you, my dear, and provide for your physical needs.*

The run-down, unkempt condition of their retirement home in Mitchell, South Dakota, bombarded his thoughts. *I suppose my inability to cook, became the determining factor in your leaving me. I know now you did not have adequate nutrition.*

Max's funeral no longer held his attention. Shad's world fell apart because of his dinner partner's funeral. With a light sob for both his Katy and for Max, Brother Shad arose, careful not to disrupt the service. He walked to the rear of the chapel, wiped his tears with the big new handkerchief given him by Matti. He ambled with measured steps down the corridor toward his room, as the receding organ strains of *It Will Be Worth It All* faded from his consciousness. Memories of happier days began to flood his mind, the birth of his daughter Tammy, the assignment to preach in his first church in Canada, and—

Where did I just come from? My handkerchief—all wet? Why? Why do I feel so upset? I must go lay down. My heart beats fast, hmm. Why did I walk down this hall? What just happened to me? I need to call Matti. She will orient me. Thank God for Matti. My mind, fuzzy again. Why? Ah, here's, my room.

THURSDAY BRUNCH AT WALDO'S
THURSDAY, AUGUST 2, 9:30 A.M.

Pete, a young pastor involved in overseas Bible school teaching, arrived at 9:30 a.m. as promised, at the front door of the Forest Building, the office and assisted-living facility for the City Center Retirement Home.

"Hi, Brother Shad," Pete exclaimed after he walked past the receptionist's desk. "Our day dawns again." Most times, while Brother Shad waited in the nearby guest room for his friend, he would sit down and talk to the small birds caged in the lobby area.

The dainty melodious creatures, ten in the new, large glass cage, provided an enjoyable attraction for residents, staff and visitors. The interaction of these tiny feathered creatures, each one no bigger than a demitasse teacup, gave pleasure to people passing through the area.

"Pete," Brother Shad smiled, "you make each Thursday special for me. On Tuesday, I begin to think about the discussion for our next rendezvous at Waldo's. These morning brunches excite me."

Thursday morning brunch for these two pastor friends from South Dakota had become a tradition. This once-a-week excursion had developed as a habit for them three years earlier. The 26 years difference in their ages created a special fondness for each other. "Do you remember, Pete, three decades earlier, we both preached and ministered in close proximity? In those days, we found time to compare notes and enjoy fellowship opportunities with our families at least once every two weeks, first at your home then at mine."

The mentor relationship transpired like father and son, teacher and student, like master craftsman and apprentice. Earlier in their lives, one man departed on an overseas missionary assignment, while the other climbed up the ministerial ladder into corporate activity of their fellowship.

As on other Thursdays, Pete greeted Brother Shad with bright eyes, a firm handshake, and a happy smile. His words illuminated their conversation: "My friend, let's cast all our 'care upon Him' for He cares for us (1 Peter 5:7)."

"For sure, Pete, we 'will be glad and rejoice in Him!' (Psalm 9:2). Scripture quotes and references framed their family-like dialogue.

"We praise and adore His worthy name."

Pete smiled, "Let us give glory to God, our strength and salvation, every day of our lives."

These types of interchanges between the two retired pastors highlighted the goodness and majesty of God each time they met. Each Thursday, the air resounded with their interplay of the Word of God and appreciation of His presence.

This morning, Brother Shad had waited for Pete near the front door. He looked forward with anticipation for Pete's arrival, who would arrange to turn off the security system for Brother Shad's ankle band and free him to leave the building. Several times each month the offensive alarm sounded at the nurses' station which signaled his escape. "Thank you for freedom from that obnoxious alarm system. I appreciate our breakfast date today."

In the last few months, Brother Shad's dementia had grown more noticeable. The nurses felt he might fall, hurt himself, walk away, or not know how to return to his room, if he were allowed to walk outside by himself.

"Punch in number 0998," Brother Shad instructed Pete. "I observed others exiting the Forest Building today. These code numbers will work for my release, too."

Brother Shad, clever and skillful in all his endeavors, learned how to punch in the code which allowed him to walk out the front door. He would look over a person's shoulder or stand behind someone who entered the code, with exit assured. The never-ending call to eradicate those yellow-hat, green-stem lawn-destroyers motivated his determination to escape.

His intent on each outdoor mission included a good walk around the grounds and a time to pull up every pesky dandelion in sight. He felt those prolific weeds caused a blight on the Center's beautiful lawns. On each sidewalk trek, his eyes surveyed every foot of grass for tell-tale signs of those hated yellow buttons.

"Pete," Brother Shad exclaimed, "I enjoy the opportunity to exercise my legs out-doors, smell the fresh air, and experience a change of scenery away from my small room. As you know, because of the sights of infirmed residents and smells of cleaning solutions in the corridors, sometimes pungent, my walks on the inside corridors do not fulfill my desire to keep my legs at maximum mobility."

Today, Pete conducted the preliminary procedures. He checked Brother Shad out at the nursing station, keyed the security touch pad, and opened the door for him. *Ah, freedom and fresh air,* Brother Shad beamed. *Escape, for our Thursday a.m. adventure, brunch at Waldo's Bread Shop and Deli.* His walk to the car took a few more minutes today. The recent corridor exercise had not supplied his need to keep good leg muscle tone.

Pete drove south on Killarney Boulevard to Waldo's, most days a ten-minute jaunt. The animated conversation continued, prompted by Brother Shad. "Pete, I thank you for your kindness. These little trips mean much to me."

"My buddy, we share the same goals: we want people to connect with Jesus. Let me tell you my good news. My granddaughter, Hannah, now age 15, gave her life to Jesus in the service last Sunday morning."

"Ooh, Pete, what great news. Praise the Lord."

"She made the decision herself after her church group viewed the *White Cane Religion* video sermon by Reverend Stephen Hill, a 1996 message from the Brownsville revival in Florida. Her teen Sunday school class watched the video as a part of a unit on career choices."

Both men discussed what young people like to do these days and what role models they might follow. When Pete drove into a space to park at Waldo's, he asked: "Brother Shad, do you like the thick, dark German bread Waldo makes?"

"I eat any kind of bread. German bread sounds delicious. Please ask the cook to make a hot chicken sandwich surrounded with lots of grapes and melon slices."

"Done. I'll order the same for myself along with two cups of hot Jamaican coffee. Sugar and cream?"

"Sugar only, thank you."

They found a booth away from the clatter of dishes and cash register sounds. Brother Shad told Pete of his recent sleep problems. "First, the new attendant walked with large clog-like shoes that clicked on the tile when he strode up and down the hall. Someone else used the floor polisher late last night. Another person sang in the garden patio area outside my window, quite off key, at seven o'clock this morning.

"I didn't sleep well. Even though tired, I couldn't turn my mind off. My daughter Tammy occupied my thoughts. I wish she would come and visit me again."

"She loves you, Brother Shad. I know she keeps busy, but I believe she will come to your room soon. I think she also misses you."

"Ah, here it comes! Brunch for a king."

"Brother Shad, will you please ask the Lord's blessing on our food and fellowship?"

The interchange progressed through different topics during the next hour, Pete checked to see how Brother Shad reacted to each of his statements and comments. He did his utmost to see that Brother Shad enjoyed their time together. Pete held his long-time friend in high esteem and knew each Thursday morning rendezvous might result in a last encounter, a last brunch together at Waldo's.

I must endeavor to encase every bit of our conversation in warm, personal, gracious thoughts and memories. Brother Shad became the father I never knew, a confidant and elder brother, a person easy to talk to, a friend forever, and a seasoned ministerial counselor. He represents an expert straight shooter with the Gospel. He never misses the mark and seldom fails to solve problems or provide solutions.

Their relationship exuded the agape love of Christ in its finest human form. Their interchange teemed with jokes, laughter, and with serious consideration of questions about ministerial matters. Each friend knew well the mind of the other.

"I need my coffee warmed up," Brother Shad noted. "This cup doesn't seem thick enough or heavy enough to hold in the heat."

"I agree," Pete volunteered. "I'll catch the waitress' eye . . . Ma'am, more java, please."

They did not use words at all times. The silence or animated conversation exhilarated both when together, whether in car rides or at a shared meal. The presence of the Holy Spirit warmed them, set up a glow in their togetherness, and prepared each with an expectancy for their next brunch and Thursday morning excursion.

"Brother Shad, I leave in four weeks to teach a three-week session in South Africa."

"What will you teach, Pete?"

"Romans and Galatians, with services each weekend."

The morning ended with their hearts full of joy and contentment for another day allowed them by the Lord. On the ride back to the Center, Brother Shad reflected: *Did we solve the problems of the world? No. Did we generate new insights garnered from God's Word? Yes. I feel I might walk on air today. I sense a renewed power surge in my legs after this trip to Waldo's. I know my afternoon nap will be sweet, restful, and relaxed without pain.*

Pete left his ministerial pal at the front door of the Center with his usual words of departure, "If the Lord allows, see you next Thursday, Dad."

"God bless you, Pete. Thank you again for the energized morning and tasty brunch."

Pete drove away, a passionate prayer on his lips: "Please, Lord, let us enjoy a few more Thursday brunches together. My special friend expresses such a sweet spirit."

Brother Shad ambled with confidence down the corridor to his room. His mind mulled over the events of their morning together: *Lord, my friend Pete displays evidence of everything working together upstairs in his head. Please place him in a suitable executive position within our fellowship.*

PART THREE

AUTUMN: CHANGES WHICH PROMPT PERSEVERANCE

But you, O LORD, are a shield for me,
My glory and the One who lifts up my head.
I cried to the LORD with my voice,
And He heard me from His Holy hill.
Selah
I lay down and slept;
I awoke, for the LORD sustained me.
Psalm 3:3–5

CHAPTER SEVEN
SECURITY QUESTIONED ABOUT FINANCES

*Therefore do not worry, saying . . . 'What shall we wear?'
For your heavenly Father knows that you need all these
things.*
Matthew 6:31, 32

LAUNDRY DAY DILEMMA
MONDAY, AUGUST 6, 8:00 A.M.

"WHERE, OH WHERE did I place my robe?" Brother Shad looked through the small closet in his room determined to find the new bathrobe given him by Tammy. With a disgusted frown and a chomp on the dentures in his mouth, he spoke out in frustration: "I can't find it. I thought I placed it by my shirts. Did I send it to the laundry? I don't think I threw it in my dirty clothes bag.

"Did someone take it without my knowledge? I don't see it on the back of my chair, not on my bed, not on a hanger in my bathroom, not on the back of the door. Where has it gone? I don't wish to walk down the corridor to the shower room in my pajamas. My scheduled shower time begins in fifteen minutes. I'm embarrassed and disgusted. Well, I know how to solve this mystery. I'll call Matti. She can help me out of this mess."

TE-da-la-DAAT-RING, ring.

"How may I help you, Brother Shad?"

"Matti, how did you know it was me?"

"The only person who calls me this early in the morning holds your phone."

"I can't find my new robe. I looked everywhere in my room. My scheduled shower time begins in fifteen minutes. I'm ashamed to walk down the corridor in my pajamas. Matti, will you please help me?"

"Pull on an old pair of pants over your pajama bottoms and go take your shower. Walk down there right away. You *must* take your shower."

"I don't like the idea, but I will do it this time. I find it offensive."

"When I come later this morning, I'll check first in the laundry room to see if your new bathrobe hangs on a rack among the clean clothes. Remember when Tammy brought it to you, she did not have an indelible ink pen to mark your name and room number on it? Perhaps I can find a reason for its non-return from the laundry room."

"Thank you, Matti. I knew you would solve my problem. I shall go take my shower. Excuse me, please."

Matti parked her car by the laundry room at 10:15 a.m. in one of the employee spaces. She justified her action: *I won't stay long, no shift changes at this time of day.* Inside the laundry facility, she noticed the staff busy with sorted and pressed clothes arranged in neat piles. Other clean pieces in the completed dry cycle of the four large commercial machines need processing.

She put on her best smile, spoke with a warm cheery voice, and inquired of Jenny, her long-time acquaintance in the wash area: "I want to locate a rather new, white wool, full-size man's bathrobe. Brother Shadrach Milburn thought he sent it to the laundry, day before yesterday, but did not mark it in the correct manner with his name and room number. Do you have anything like that in your pile of unidentified items?"

"Yes, Matti. Come over here," Jenny answered with a motion of her hands. "Check this garment hung at the end of the rack. Does it fit your description?"

"For sure, the lost bathrobe—found. Jenny, may I take it to Brother Shad? I brought my marker pen today. We won't let it happen again."

"Okay, Matti," Jenny replied in a curt manner. "The Lord bless your day. Sorry I can't talk longer. On Mondays," she turned to walk away, "we scramble to complete our laundry duties during shift time."

"Many thanks, Jenny." Matti clasped her hands together around the bathrobe, then waved goodbye as she exited. "The Lord bless you, too."

A FAMILY COURT SESSION

Knock, knock!

"Come in, Matti, and welcome to my one-room office, home and parlor."

"Good day, Reverend Milburn."

"Please be seated, madam," Brother Shad smiled at Aunt Matti's courteousness and air of politeness. She greeted him with professional respect, developed from years of association with administrators, students and church families. He, too, acted like a gentleman, no matter what situation might transpire.

"I found your bathrobe in the laundry facility a few minutes ago. No one knew to whom it belonged because it had no marks." She took the marker pen out of her purse and looked at him with expectation. "Let's mark it now. The ink can dry before you put it on tonight."

"Matti, I shall forever call you a special person." He gave a sigh of relief. "Whatever would I do without your concern for me each day?" He hung up the bathrobe on his clothes rack and said with a big smile, "You qualify as more than a dear friend."

"Did you shower this morning?" she inquired in a soft voice.

"Yes, wore my trousers over my pajamas to hide my embarrassment."

"Did you put on clean underwear and socks?"

"Yes, Mom."

"Did you put on a clean sport shirt?"

"Yes, General."

Matti knew the habits of how men dressed, so she continued her examination. "Did you place your dirty underwear, socks, and shirt in the clothes bag?"

"Aye, aye, Sir."

"Did you shave this morning?"

"No, I didn't feel like it."

You look like an old man when you don't shave."

"I am an old man."

"Why don't you shave every day?"

"Guess I'm lazy."

"You look younger when you shave." She knew how to spur her old friend into a complete clean up job each morning.

"Humph!"

"Have your read your Bible this morning?"

"Of course, Professor!"

"What did you read?"

"Luke, Chapters one through ten, Your Honor."

"Have you had time to pray?"

"Only for Tammy, Melody, and you, Pastor."

Her interrogation required skill and perception of his changing moods. Matti never knew how Brother Shad might react to daily situations he encountered at the Center. He might act confused. At other times he interacted with her, like this time, with wit and humor. She never knew when his high blood pressure might cause another loss of memory episode.

"Court dismissed," Aunt Matti chuckled. "Class cancelled, but will resume tomorrow. If the doctor will excuse me, please, I shall call on two other friends at the Center this morning."

"Okay, Matti. Bless you again for your prompt assistance." He patted her arm in appreciation, "I don't know what you did, but thank you again for retrieving my bathrobe."

"I will stop by later this afternoon, after your nap. We'll walk together around the corridor. Even though you may have walked the corridors by that time, we'll do it again. You *must* continue to exercise."

He knew Matti was right, but didn't want to admit it. "Goodbye until later, helpful lady."

"Bye, Prince." She spoke fondly and signaled her intent with a raised hand.

The prince of preachers sat down in his dilapidated lounge chair after he escorted Matti to his open door. His eyes did not focus on Luke Chapter 11 in the open Bible on his lap. Instead, he prayed: "Dear, Lord, I'm pleading again. Please take me home. I feel so alien here in this Retirement Center. Can I not walk the streets of gold and talk with You? Can You not use me somehow in heaven? I desire Your accommodations. Why must I wait? My old body seems worn out? However, by Your decision, I shall stand by, ready for Your call."

"ARE MY BILLS PAID?"
TUESDAY, AUGUST 7, 10:30 A.M.

"Matti," Brother Shad said as he searched every pocket in his pants and shirt, "I can not find any money in my pockets. How can I pay for my meals and monthly lodging? I hope they won't throw me out. Where would I go? What would I do? Please tell me about my finances. Do I have anything in my savings and checking accounts?" His voice increased in volume as he rose out of his chair. "What are my balances? Who pays my bills at the Center?"

Brother Shad's face turned red, his breathing grew rapid. Every six weeks like clockwork, he worried about his finances. It upset his demeanor for the entire day. Of the many problems for which he called Matti, the lack of money perplexed him most.

She had received his frantic telephone call at 7:45 a.m. and once again exerted extreme patience for another one of his "no money" encounters. "I could not come earlier when you telephoned, because I received three lengthy calls. One call came from the Philippines."

"Thank you for coming, Matti." He often stated his 'thank yous' in groups of threes. "I looked through my dresser drawers. I can't find anything about my financial payments to the Center. Who pays my bills?" Brother Shad spoke wide-eyed, rubbing his hands together in a frenzy. "What financial resources do I hold? What bank manages my funds? I cannot find a statement about these monthly transactions. Matti," he pleaded, "please tell me about my accounts."

"Your accounts remain safe," she replied in slow measured tones. "A monthly deduction from your bank account pays for your room, board, laundry bill, and medical expenses with an automatic debit scheduled through the business office and in cooperation with your bank. The Social Security agency deposits funds each month into your bank account," she continued, legs crossed as she sat on a wooden chair, her hand on his arm.

"Your minister's retirement fund sends a monthly stipend to the bank. The business office at the Center receives payments from your medical insurance. Your long-term care premiums are credited to the correct account. All your accounts tally," she smiled. "Your money will last a long time."

"I knew I could count on you, Matti." He sighed with relief. You watch over my accounts well, just like you did forty years ago at the minister's central office. You set up our district bookkeeping, and now you continue that diligent practice for me. With you in charge of my finances, I feel confident. I can relax. Thank you."

"Brother Shad, I check your bank account each month. Everything is in order," she asserted. "You can sleep all night long tonight, no need to toss and turn."

"I feel like you lifted a heavy burden from my shoulders. I feel I can breathe easier." He relaxed and said, "The day looks brighter. Uh, Matti, why did you come this morning? Shall we go out again for ice cream and coffee?

"I'm having a sudden headache! Not intense, just a dull pain, a throb around the right side and close to my forehead. Maybe I should lie down for a while."

"You rest a few minutes, then we'll go out for a snack. For now, just breathe slowly and deeply. I'll sit in your chair." Within moments, Brother Shad fell asleep accompanied by heavy breathing, his financial concerns dismissed for another time.

Aunt Matti looked out his partially opened window, watched the goldfish in the nearby garden pond, and smelled the fragrance of new-mown grass. Her gaze surveyed the bees which darted for nectar among the garden flowers. *There must be a hive nearby,* she concluded.

Humming birds fluttered around bugle-bell like blossoms and sought their morning snack. A robin cocked his head, watched, and listened for insect and worm sounds in the thick lush grass planted around the stair-stepped garden pond.

I believe my friend occupies the best room in the Center complex. The Lord provided life around him in what otherwise might exist as a sterile environment. This beautiful sight gives him longevity and provides relaxation. I know these more tranquil scenes help reduce his stress. 'Lord, please don't let Brother Shad suffer another stroke, even little ones that cause him headaches.'

Aunt Matti prayed often whenever a moment like this presented itself. She settled herself down into Shad's worn chair, which allowed her to contemplate his present condition, reflect on their past association, and consider his possible future developments. Her prayers turned into daydreams, and in moments those daydreams developed into a light sleep. This time, the panorama included her husband Dan, who had begun to court her back in their Bible school days.

He described her as "Jesus' little sunbeam," whenever he spoke to their friends and colleagues about his interest in her. She felt Dan a jovial person, albeit a bit mischievous, an intellectual fellow, but a down-to-earth guy, a fine singer and a persistent suitor. Not having a car, he asked, "Shall we walk over to the zoo? I enjoy watching the peacocks and giraffes."

"Okay. The exercise will help both of us," Matti would reply. On their walks to the zoo, she sometimes remarked, "I think completion of Bible school shows a person's ability to sit for long periods of time. I wonder if the administration gives us course credit just because of our seat time in class?"

"Naw," Dan replied. Seat time in class means boys can meet girls and receive credit for exposure to the whims of the female gender."

"One more crack like that, Dan, and I'll ask the zoo keeper to put you in a cage. In fact, I'll find my own way home today. Good bye."

Their senior year at Bible school, however, brought them together into a relationship filled with dates and weekend ministry in a nearby small town. Matti played the piano. Dan sang, lead worship, and he often rendered a vocal solo for each service.

"What song did you choose for this Sunday morning service?" Matti asked one day.

"I feel *Friendship with Jesus* will help prepare the people's hearts for my message entitled: *Blind Bartimaeus Believed* from Mark 10:46-52." Dan's voice rang crystal-clear, a lyrical tenor. He phrased well, varied his dynamics, did not strain on the higher notes, nor did he sound mushy on the lower passages.

His middle range projected mellowness. His renditions excited parishioners with the varied tempos, clear enunciation, and accuracy evidenced by good breath support. A person knew after the first phrase he possessed a trained voice.

"Please keep your special solo, *I'm His to Command,* on the ready," Matti requested, her eyes glowing with admiration. She advised, "I think this Bible-believing congregation will enjoy both songs on Sunday. Both fit into your sermon. However, I like the message of your favorite ballad. It clearly tells everyone, when we give our talents and lives to the Lord, He will lead us and use us every day for His purposes and His glory."

Matti's recollections continued of her early college music ministry with Dan. He interpreted songs in a way that left members wanting an encore, whenever he sang their favorites like *How Great Thou Art* or *It Was Love for Me* or *The Name of Jesus Is So Sweet.* His youthful praise of the Lord encouraged their adoration of the Savior. His exaltation of the name of Jesus in services caused joyous and intimate worship of the Lord.

Aunt Matti, self-taught in the craft of piano performance, learned the basics from her father, who capitalized on her natural talent and persistent desire to excel. She learned to follow any vocalist in sensitive changes of a phrase, expression, and pace.

"Dan, you and I ministered like a well-groomed team. We moved together in the Spirit, sensed the mood of a song, and the receptivity of listeners. This combination served us well through many years of ministry in churches, camp meetings, at weddings and community affairs."

"Matti!"

She felt her eyes were closed only a second. "Oh my!" a check of her watch, indicated a half hour had passed.

"Matti, don't you think it's time for ice cream? My mouth feels dry. Guess I dozed with my mouth open. I need something to cool my throat. How about another trip to Dolly's?"

AN ICE CREAM EXCURSION INTERRUPTED

"Yes, Brother Shad, I'm ready. I need a good meal. My light breakfast snack will not carry me through the day. I ate less than usual because I hurried to come see you. Why don't we go to the Fish 'n Steak House. It sounds like a $16-per-plate classy restaurant, but it serves moderate-to-low-income people. I went there last week with my niece. You'll like it. They serve nutritious meals at modest prices."

"For this outing, I must run a comb through my hair. . . . Okay, Driver, I'm ready. Show me the way."

As the two friends walked toward the front entrance, he hinted: "I hope they serve hot coffee. The aide did not bring me any hot coffee today. My breakfast this morning arrived cold."

"I'm sure the restaurant will serve us well. When we ate there last week, several college-age young people served as waiters. They looked clean cut and ready to please. A nice young man waited on our table, a sophomore in the physics department. I believe you will enjoy the home-like—"

Crash! Thud!

"Brother Shad," Aunt Matti looked down and shouted. "What happened? What's wrong?"

He tried to sit up from his fallen position, but with hesitation replied: "I, my knees, like rubber. I, blacked out. My heart feels like a jack hammer in my chest. Matti, please call the nurse for me. My head aches. Everything—spins and spins."

Thud!

He collapsed to the floor again. Aunt Matti spoke nervously to the receptionist, Mrs. Penderholt. "Let's straighten out Brother Shad on the floor." It took a few seconds because of his large body. Within minutes the nursing staff rushed down the hall with their emergency equipment piled on the top of a gurney.

"I'm Nurse Hotchkiss. What happened to Brother Shad?"

"We started to go out for lunch," Aunt Matti exclaimed. "Brother Shad collapsed, twice. The first time he complained of a headache and dizziness."

"Let me check his vital signs before we move him. Hmm . . . pulse weak and irregular.

Oh my, very low blood pressure. Okay, the three of you here, go around to that side; you three stand on this side. I'll hold his head while we lift him on to the gurney. Altogether now on the count of three: one, two, three, up. Careful there . . . together, together. Okay, strap him down so he doesn't fall off."

Nurse Hotchkiss' questions did not receive the answers she desired to hear. She wondered: *Did Brother Shad take his blood pressure medicine this morning? I shall investigate his records after we return him to his room.*

Brother Shad groaned softly with increased intensity and struggled against the straps on his legs, waist, and chest. "Where am I? What happened?" he asked. "Why am I on this bed in the corridor? Matti, where—"

"I'm right beside you, dear friend. My hand holds your wrist. Can you feel my hand?"

"Yes. Matti, but I can't see well. My eyes don't focus. Ouch! My head still aches."

"Try to relax. We will go back to your room. Nurse Hotchkiss will check on your medications. Did you take your blood pressure medicine this morning?"

"I don't remember. I'm not sure. Look in my waste basket. If you see a paper cup there, yes; if not, no. Gregory takes out my trash at suppertime."

"Nothing there, Brother Shad." Aunt Matti's face felt flushed. She grew concerned about her friend's slow recovery.

With Brother Shad back in his bed, Nurse Hotchkiss volunteered, "I'll check the nurses' station record for him." She displayed no emotion. "I employed a new aide for this wing today. We may soon know the cause for Brother Shad's sudden collapse. Brother Shad, do not get up. Lie on your bed for a few minutes. I'll return in a few minutes, check your pulse and monitor your blood pressure."

Nurse Hotchkiss turned around, head erect, shoulders back. She exited the room with her all-business attitude, eyes focused toward the nurses' station.

"I imagine," remarked Aunt Matti to Brother Shad, "one new aide may see her last day in the Center today."

"Matti, I must pray for that young girl. She meant me no harm. 'Father, in the name of Jesus, we claim Your mind and provision for the new aide. If, indeed, she caused my collapse, Lord, spare her. Please help her to do good work and learn reliable techniques. Thank You, Jesus.'"

Nurse Hotchkiss returned and entered the door, face flushed, her emotions upset as Brother Shad finished his short prayer. "Mister Milburn, take these pills you did not receive at breakfast. You may sit up, but take your time. Let me help you. Do not stand, just sit and swallow. Drink . . . take your time. Good. Now lie back down, in slow motion. I want you to close your eyes and rest for a while. I will bring lunch to your room in about an hour."

CHAPTER EIGHT

SPACE SHARED WITH OTHERS

*Comfort the fainthearted, uphold the weak,
be patient with all.*
1 Thessalonians 5:14

INVASION OF MY PRIVACY
FRIDAY, AUGUST 10, 8:30 A.M.

THE OUTSIDER KNOCKED ON Brother Shad's door, breaking the retired minister's thought while he read his Bible. "Excuse me, please. Can you tell me in which room Teresa Hilmstead lives?"

"Turn left, third door on the right," the aged pastor motioned and chomped his false teeth together in repeated annoyance while he looked over the top of his glasses at the intruder who had interrupted his concentration.

"Thank you, Sir, and have a good day."

Brother Shad's eyes returned to the open Bible on his lap. He sighed, shook his head in disgust, and continued to read: "It is a fearful thing to fall into the hands of the living God" (Hebrews 10:31). He felt excited by the Book of Hebrews, but disturbed by the bleak outlook for sinners made clear in Chapter10:29-31.The three stated ways a person could turn his back on God caused the old gentleman consternation.

Because thereafter, no method of return to the Lord or acceptance of His provision for salvation could be found in this passage. Thus he read out loud for the fifth time, Hebrews 10:29: "Of how much worse punishment, do you suppose, will he be thought worthy who has trampled the Son of God underfoot, counted the blood of the covenant by which he was sanctified a common thing, and insulted the Spirit of grace?"

"Father, I understand this passage to mean: if a person considers Jesus Christ as contaminated dirt under someone's feet, and the power of His shed blood no better than putrid sewer water, and the actuality of guidance by the Holy Spirit nothing more than a fairy tale, then a doomed life in hell would become that person's eternal future.

"'Lord, I pray one more time for my two fellow pastors who stooped to this impossible and despicable level of depravity last year. Somehow bring them both back to You. Lord, intervene in their lives. In Your sovereignty, forgive them, reclaim them, and rehabilitate them for Your glory. Amen.' For I believe Jesus, that you mean a person who accepts this philosophy of degradation and state of godless existence will live like an animated dead corpse. Jesus—"

Another voice at his open door burst into his concentration, "Hi, Sammy. Oh, excuse me. You're not Sammy. I seek my boy, Sammy. He comes today to take me home. You know, we live up in St. Paul."

"Theda, look in the activities room. You might see him there."

"Oh, thank you, young man. Sorry to bother you. Say, do you play checkers?"

"No, Theda."

"Bye young fellow, and don't forget to blow your nose." With that disruptive intrusion, she backed her wheelchair out of the aged pastor's doorway, kept up the conversation with herself, and moved down the corridor. In her hurry, she forgot all about Sammy, and disappeared into the activities room.

Once again the eyes of the old man focused on his open Bible. This time he read Hebrews 10:38: "Now the just shall live by faith; But if anyone draws back, My soul has no pleasure in him."

Knock, Knock.

These people must think I'm a ticket agent.

"Good morning, Brother Shad. Please swallow your morning pill and drink your special shake." This morning, Nurse Hotchkiss strode through his doorway unannounced, intent on the performance of her regular delivery. She left no indecision about the recipient's course of action.

"Yes, Ma'am!" Obedience meant everything with Nurse Hotchkiss who expected immediate compliance.

Everyone on the floor knew the rules. To argue in any way with Nurse Hotchkiss might mean banishment to the Alzheimer's unit in the "other" building. Brother Shad did not wish to give up his small room with its window facing the fish pond in the nearby patio. The outdoor scenery in the patio gave him a sense of peace and tranquility in a world in which he found it most difficult to share space with other residents.

Nurse Hotchkiss wasted no motion. Before the student of the Bible finished his shake, she moved to the next room. She knew he would complete the necessary routine.

That Nurse Hotchkiss, a fine woman. I wonder, Brother Shad pondered as he finished his special shake, *if she has grandchildren?* He watched a large, black crow peck in the grass outside his window as he contemplated the lifestyle of this lady: "In what kind of family did she grow up? She means business, always strict, but she gives good care. Well, I've finished my Bible reading for this session.

"I think I need to pray for this kind lady. 'Holy Spirit, You prompted me to pray for Nurse Hotchkiss and her family. Please keep Your hand upon her; guide her. Don't let her make mistakes. Bless her. In Jesus' name.'"

A VISIT BY TAMMY AND MELODY

"Hi, Dad." Tammy peeked around the corner of his doorway.

"Hi, Grandpa." Melody raised a hand in greeting, while unbuttoning the top part of her sweater.

"Hello, my dears." This intrusion caused him to sit up straight. He gave them both a big smile while motioning them to come in and sit down.

"What did you read this morning," Tammy queried, "Revelation or John?"

"Neither. I reviewed Hebrews, chapters one through ten."

"Grandpa, do you ever become tired when you read those Bible passages?"

"Never, Sweetie. It keeps me close to Jesus and confirms to me He lives."

"Dad, we came out today to bring you new winter socks and a wool sweater. Both items should keep you comfortable in the cooler weather forecast in about four weeks. Do you like the sweater? Please try it on. We think you'll look nice in greenish plaid. It buttons down the front and has a pocket on each side."

With assistance from Melody, he put on the sweater and fastened the lower two buttons. "It feels good, snug and warm. Beautiful. I like it. Thank you, girls."

Whirrr, whirrr, whirrr!

"Excuse me please, Brother Shad, I must buff the floor. A change of occupants occurred last night in the room across the corridor from yours. Before the new resident moves in after lunch today, we must finish the clean-up and sanitize the room. Thank you, sir, for your patience and willingness to understand."

The custodian, Wilfred, worked hard. Known as a gracious man, he carried a little extra weight, but displayed a gracious heart when confronted with these challenges. He tried his best to minimize interruptions in the resident's schedules. Situations like this tended to cause stress for persons in nearby rooms.

"Close the door, Melody," Tammy spoke, as she looked in the direction of the buffer. Dad, I think we should call this interruption a good time to find a dish of mint chocolate-chip ice cream not too far away. Everyone in favor raise your hand . . . anyone opposed? Three in favor, no dissentions, no abstentions. Let's do it."

The three walked down the corridor arm-in-arm toward the receptionist's desk. Mrs. Penderholt glanced up from her computer. "Brother Shad, I'm so glad you're here. Something happened with these birdies. They screeched and flitted about, upset in their cage this morning. Will you pray for them, please, like you did before? You're the best bird man in the Center."

"What seems to cause the problem, Mrs. Penderholt?"

"I think two of our birds hover near death. Those two who sit on the floor, on that far side look like they want to shrivel up. Please pray for them, Brother Shad. I know their health will return after you pray."

"All right, but look," he said as he bent over near the end of the panel-truck-size bird cage. "I see one tiny egg under the breast of the bird on the right and two eggs under a wing of the other. Wow, so tiny. I think the delivery of the eggs can best describe the problem for these two. However, let's pray.

"Father, in the name of Jesus, please help these two small creatures in Your bird kingdom to deliver whatever more teensy-weensy eggs may reside in their bodies without further complications. Help them to incubate and hatch beautiful baby birds that will add to the enjoyment of the staff and residents, and to this small flock in the cage.

"Keep Your hand upon them. Heal their bodies, we pray. And, may all these birds sing again soon with their gorgeous melodies and blended harmony. In Jesus' mighty name, I pray. Amen."

"Brother Shad, your prayer did it," Mrs. Penderholt squealed as she clapped her hands. "Look, they settled down. Bless You, Lord." Mrs. Penderholt, an unemotional person, saw *her birdie's* behavior return to normal as a miracle. It brought out the pleasant side of her personality.

While the prayer meeting had been in progress, Theda moved her wheelchair near the door. "I want to find my boy, Sammy. He plans to take us home to St. Paul. Did anyone see him come in?"

"No, Theda," Brother Shad answered in a cordial manner.

"Well, tell him if you see him, I will wait for him in the activities room. Sorry to bother you. Say, young man, do you play checkers?"

"No, Theda."

"Bye, everybody. Don't forget, young fella, to blow your nose." With that out-of-context comment, she turned her wheelchair around and continued her one-sided monologue. No longer concerned about Sammy or playing a game of checkers, she wheeled herself down the corridor.

"Look, Mom," Melody said, gazing out the front window of the reception lobby "It's Aunt Matti by the front-door buzzer."

"Push the automatic door opener, Melody, and let her come in." Tammy's smile glowed

"Hello, my fine octogenarian caregiver," Brother Shad exclaimed. He stood up straight on his weak legs and said: "We shall depart in one minute for a dish of ice cream. Will you join us?"

"Thank you for the invitation, but I must visit three people this morning. One of the three, the mother of a friend who died here last night, needs my support and reassurance. I feel it appropriate for me to spend time with her this morning. You three seldom manage time together as a family. Brother Shad, you and I can go another time. You three enjoy the day together."

Aunt Matti did not often act with abruptness in her interactions with people, but she foresaw a busy day for herself. In the afternoon she planned to attend a funeral and go to her bank later to draw out a few dollars which she kept on hand for those times when a restaurant would not accept her check. "Please forgive me for the rush." She walked away, raising a hand to wave a cordial goodbye.

DOLLY'S ICE CREAM PARLOR

The excursion to Dolly's Ice Cream Parlor gave Brother Shad an opportunity to escape the hustle-bustle of busy staff duties on his wing and the confusion of some residents in nearby rooms. His frustration included late meals in the dining room, food he did not always care to eat, and the invasion of his privacy by unwelcome residents. These family excursions helped him keep a balanced perspective about his daily routine.

"Melody," Brother Shad declared to his granddaughter as he turned his head and pointed to the scene around their car. "On these short trips, I enjoy the sun, the trees, and an acceptable escape from the four walls of my room. Do take time, young lady, to enjoy God's provision of nature around us."

"I know you were a preacher, Grandpa, but I feel you still think like a cowboy, because of where you grew up. You notice things that I do not consciously think of, like the way the rainwater flows on a street. Or like the proverb I learned last week, 'Red sky in the morning, sailors take warning; red sky at night, sailors delight.'"

The animated conversation between granddaughter and grandfather stopped momentarily when they drove into Dolly's parking lot. As they entered the ice cream shop, Brother Shad thought again about heaven. *Jesus, will today be my day? Dear Lord, sometimes I think I live in a zoo, a human stockyard. Please don't tarry. Jesus, come soon.*

Tammy noticed the rush of customers had not yet assembled as the waitress brought glasses of water to their table. "Dad," would you like a bowl of chili to complement your ice cream and coffee?"

"Yes, I do feel a bit hungry. I will enjoy that combination today."

Melody leaned up against her grandpa as they sat beside each other and began to eat their chili. "Do many people come visit in your room?"

"No, dear, not many. I can count on one hand the few people who stop by to visit in any two-week period. Most of my visitors hold positions on the nursing and custodial staff. The fellows I eat with in the dining room serve as my closest friends." He clicked his dentures together several times in order to remove a piece of lumpy meat from his gums.

"The other people around here don't take time to socialize. Their own responsibilities keep them busy. This type of interaction reminds me of robots, a job must be completed in eight hours, and a responsibility enacted, then checked off the list."

"Mom," Melody asked while she savored another small bite of her hamburger, "how do you compare Grandpa's relationships at the Center to yours at the Library? Does the staff have good personal relationships among your associates or do many employees just put in the necessary time for their jobs?"

"I believe our Library workers care about each other." With her napkin, she wiped a drop of catsup from the corner of her mouth. "We try to help visitors, no matter what age level, whenever a request for assistance comes across our desks. Sometimes a request will involve two or three of us, such as three fourth graders working on a research project describing the Great Salt Lake. Dad's situation requires people with wider ranges of talent who have different types of responsibilities, unlike our Library skill requirements."

Brother Shad saw an opportunity to work on Melody's social skills. He exhorted, "Remember the people you work with make the difference between success or stress on the job. Some days proceed well, other days may erupt in turmoil." He looked at one person then the other, "Each one of us must work to help our associates and colleagues enjoy and produce a good day of work."

"Grandpa said it right, Melody." Tammy used both hands to express, "Be a 'giver' and project a positive outlook on life. Shy away from the 'takers.' Don't let them drain you of your spiritual energy, your spiritual resiliency in Christ."

Melody took in all their recommendations, then looked at her watch in alarm. "Mom, look at the time. I don't want to be late for band practice. Will you drop me off, please, before taking Grandpa back to the Center?"

"For sure," she smiled. "Ready, Dad, for a round-about car ride?"

FOOD DOESN'T EXCITE ME
SUNDAY, AUGUST 12, 5:OO P.M.

Matti hurried to Shad's room. She wanted to assist him in his preparation for the Sunday evening rally. "Brother Shad, we cannot go to the chapel service this evening if you don't eat your supper," Aunt Matti scolded.

His folded arms enforced his determination to enjoy only ice cream and hot coffee three times each day. He ground his teeth in annoyance and replied, "I'm not hungry."

"You need protein to keep up your strength. You cannot walk the corridors or even go outside with friends unless you eat solid food."

"I don't want their food." The aged minister responded in a stubborn manner. A person would think he dug his heels into the cement floor while seated in his lounge chair. He refused to budge. His recalcitrant attitude called up all the persuasiveness Aunt Matti could muster. This time she found it more difficult than ever to persuade the old fellow to eat at least a small portion of his supper.

One time before, she encouraged him to eat when she said: "the food you eat will ward off the spring coolness of our walk into the church downtown." Another time she talked him into consuming a meal by saying: "Let's divide this chicken sandwich. I'll share it with you." On one occasion, when at Dolly's she said, "The sugar in the ice cream you eat will burn up fast and leave you without sufficient energy to read your Bible."

"The food on my tray doesn't do anything for me." He wrinkled his face, "It's tasteless."

"What kind of food do you like to eat?" Matti's concerned look bore through his attempted defense.

"This does not resemble home-cooked food. It provides no satisfying taste. It needs more salt and a few savory spices."

"Did you eat your breakfast this morning?" she asked politely.

"Only a few mouthfuls."

"Why only a few mouthfuls?"

"I wasn't hungry," he spoke with disdain.

"Brother Shad, why don't you tell me everything that bothers you. What was wrong with the breakfast fare?" Matti leaned forward and placed a finger on his forearm.

"Tasteless, cold, looks like leftovers warmed up."

"I find that hard to believe. The Center tries to take good care of its residents. What do you mean, 'your breakfast came tasteless, cold, and looked like leftovers warmed up?'"

"Matti, I feel tired of life," he sighed. I can't hear all words in a conversation. My mind doesn't function well. My memory doesn't exist anymore." Inhaling deeply, he continued, "I want Jesus to come for me!"

"Instead of our walk to the chapel service this evening, let's talk about your feelings about food. Okay, my friend?"

With folded arms, he concluded, "I'm content to sit right here until Jesus comes for me."

"Do you remember, Jesus told us in Luke 19:13: 'Occupy till I come.' (KJV) What did He mean?"

"Matti, I no longer desire to serve or minister to invalids in my small way at the Center. I can't have a good conversation with anyone, but you. My memory flew away," He emphasized his frustration with a flip of his right hand toward the ceiling. "I don't feel on top of things. I lost control of small activities in my life some time ago. For example, where did I place my socks? Did I put on a clean sport shirt for the day?" He slouched in desperation. "It makes me feel like my self-worth evaporated; my self-confidence flew out the window."

"Brother Shad, depression bothers you because you don't eat your meals," she spoke with motherly compassion. "You have plenty of money in your account, You need not scrimp by failing to eat and thereby think you save money. The total package charge for your room and utility fees includes your meals."

"I don't like to eat by myself. When we go together to a restaurant, I don't mind a small amount of food, but I don't want to gain weight. I'm not happy, just sad. No Katy, no memory, no strong legs," his hands flailed the air as if he spoke to a deaf person. "No regular friends come to visit, no outside walks, and my false teeth don't work well."

"Are you applying dental paste to both dentures each morning," she asked respectfully, "to help the teeth stick to your jaw and gums?"

"No," he said as he diverted his attention out the window away from Matti.

"Why not?"

"It's too much bother. Halfway through the noon meal my teeth slip and slid around in my mouth. Seeds stick beneath my store-bought teeth and irritate my gums and jaw. I can't chew well. Only soft foods seem edible for me. I can't sink these store-bought teeth into a fine steak. These dentures just don't work well." He spoke in quick phrases. "After I use the dental paste at noon, my dentures come loose again by suppertime."

"The Lord expects you to take care of yourself, Brother Shad. Remember, 1 Corinthians 6:19, our 'body is the temple of the Holy Spirit.' We must take care of it, which includes feeding it to keep it in good shape. You may need a new set of teeth, because of a problem in a gum area."

"That costs too much, too expensive."

"I suggest you call Tammy and ask her to schedule a date with your dentist to check the condition of your dentures." Matti wasn't sure how far she might continue this train of thought with her aging friend. She observed a lessening of his patience with her continued interrogation.

"That would be a waste of money. It would cost too much. I don't want to use what money I may have to buy an unneeded luxury." Shad's voice grew louder and more persistent.

"A good set of teeth would help you chew the food and allow you to enjoy your meals. Consider a set of good dentures an asset. It would not be a luxury; it would be a help for your emotional well-being and your outlook on life. If you can't eat, your health will deteriorate."

Matti decided to pursue a more feminine approach to his dilemma. "I don't wish to see that happen and I don't think Tammy and Melody would feel comfortable to see you sick or infirm."

"My mind doesn't dwell on food. I live in a fog." A small tear formed in the corner of his eye, "I'm not sure what to do next in my day. More and more I lose contact with my familiar routine at the Center. I must verbalize my basic habits these days in order to maintain at least partial control of my life."

"Brother Shad, help me review in my mind what kind of food you enjoy. What main dishes interest you? What can you chew? Do you enjoy beef?"

"No, too tough."

"Chicken?"

"Okay, if cut into small pieces and perhaps placed in a casserole."

"Fish?"

"Some, not the smelly kind."

"Ham?" *At least he stills speaks with me. I believe we have a breakthrough.*

"No, I despise ham. The Israelites didn't eat ham nor the Jews today. I can't chew it."

"Turkey?" "Yes, with all the trimmings and side dishes. Once a week would be splendid."

"Spaghetti and meatballs?"

"No, they serve it cold in the dining room and," he leaned forward to emphasize his feelings, "with few meatballs."

"Will you eat pizza?"

"Yes, if made with a thin crust, but without ham or beef."

"I suggest, Brother Shad, we go to Dolly's Ice Cream Parlor for a chicken sandwich and a cup of coffee. May I take you for lunch this evening? *I hope he agrees. I have no more options.* We could continue this discussion over some acceptable food."

"Yes, I don't think my calendar shows any other appointments." He appreciated the release of tension from her aggressive questioning. "Nor do I have any options," he added. "And will you add a small dish of ice cream to my order, please?"

"Of course," she stood and adjusted her sleeveless sweater, "will do!"

Their discussion over Brother Shad's distaste for food and his inability to chew hard food continued at Dolly's as they ate their chicken sandwiches. Sitting knee-to-knee in a small booth, Matti gave him a compassionate smile, "My fellow South Dakotan, even though you have attained 94 years and five months, several people look to you for guidance, support, and counsel."

Brother Shad grasped the lead in their conversation. "Matti, I'm worn-out. I forget the name of the person with whom I may engage in conversation." He spoke quietly with downcast eyes. "Embarrassment describes my emotional state when that happens."

Aunt Matti peered straight into Brother Shad's eyes without a blink while she spoke. "Tammy, Melody, and I look to you for emotional support each day. Your presence fills a void in each of our lives not possible by any other male. Christians call it family." She spoke tenderly. "You know the specific truth of what I speak."

"I want to check out." He pushed his empty dishes to the side of the table. "Nobody here needs my help."

"When that time comes, we shall miss you. But until that time ordained by God, your smile, warm greetings, discernment, and wisdom remain appreciated more than you realize by the three of us, by your resident friends, and by the staff members. Your presence exudes warmth and Christ's love to those around you. Brother Shad," Matti ventured a final request, "please take care of yourself and eat the food prepared for you at the Center."

"I will take your suggestions under advisement." *And God,* he prayed silently, *help me to be cognizant of Your plan for my life, even in my old age. Lord Jesus, even though my memory continues to diminish, please don't let me become senile, cantankerous, or hard to live with.*

"Keep placing one foot ahead of the other," Matti advised as she stood up, their meal now completed. "Pick 'em up, put 'em down; move forward in the Lord. We celebrate the victory in Jesus. Don't let the evil one deceive you. With every breath, don't forget to praise and thank Him for your blessings of each day."

"Dear friend, I know you mean well and speak the truth." Standing up, he held her hands for a brief moment. "But now, please take me home. My heavy eyelids tell me my bed time beckons."

CHAPTER NINE

STRONG MEMORIES OF YESTER YEAR

*Be sober, reverent, temperate,
sound in faith, in love, in patience.*
Titus 2:2

"I AM NOT DEAF"
SUNDAY, AUGUST 19, 11:00 A.M.

MELODY WHISPERED, "WAKE UP, Grandpa. I tapped your arm three times. Please don't fall asleep and offend Chaplain Sinclair. You might snore while he preaches this morning."

"Humph! Pinch my arm, Melody, if it happens again. I didn't sleep well last night. I dreamt a violent snowstorm with cold winds hit our Canadian farm near Weyburn. We secured the cattle and horses in our barns. The two hired hands remained on standby to protect the animals and keep them calm.

"Someone, however, knocked at our back door. We went to investigate several times, but no one there. No tracks, no car in the driveway, no horse and buggy tethered by the shed. The dream bothered me most of the night. I tossed and turned, broke out in a sweat, and didn't go to sleep until early this morning after I cried out to Jesus for help."

Melody whispered to her grandfather, careful to not interrupt the service. "Let me hold your hand, Grandpa. I will squeeze it if I see your head tip and you start to doze."

"Good idea. I do want to hear Chaplain Sinclair. But the dream still haunts me. I shall rebuke old Slew-foot, the evil one, again. I remember we enjoyed a dynamic revival service the Sunday before that storm.

"I still recall the event. Many young people gave their lives to the Lord at a particular service. I imagine the enemy Satan wanted someone from our home out on the farm to go out in the storm for some reason that night and get lost, never to return. The devil hated the fact young people accepted Christ in this revival."

Curiosity overcame his need for sleep. Perplexing thoughts in Brother Shad's mind blotted out concentration on Chaplain Sinclair's sermon. *Why did I dream last night about that snowstorm so many years ago? I must ask Jesus about my dream. He may reveal His answer to me in another dream, maybe toni . . .*

"Grandpa, wake up," Melody whispered again. "The sermon will conclude in a few minutes. Reverend Sinclair may call on you for a closing prayer. Please be alert."

Even as Melody squeezed his hand several times during the message, the old man found concentration difficult. He could not hear the speaker clearly. The headset on his ears squealed on occasion; reception remained fuzzy. *Needs a new battery,* he decided. *I wish Reverend Sinclair would speak louder. I hear perhaps no more than twenty-five percent of what he says.*

Melody perceived her grandfather evidenced a hearing problem, but didn't realize the acuteness of his condition until the service this morning. "Grandpa . . . Grandpa." Melody spoke a little louder afterward, then looked straight at her grandfather while they sat beside each other in the pew. "Did your headset receiver work this morning?"

"No, my dear. I understood very little of the sermon. I'm not deaf." His demeanor changed to resignation. "I just can't hear well anymore."

This last interchange revealed the extent of Brother Shad's hearing problem. After he gave the headset and battery pack to the attendant at the back of the chapel, the two buddies walked unhurried toward the aged minister's room. Hand in hand, their center of attention focused on the pictures hung on the corridor walls.

"I like this one best," Melody remarked, pointing to the texture and background of the tall grass on the hillside. "The lion and the lamb that lay down together, both friends, not enemies. I see life in the wooded area. It preserves the pastoral scene, like cattle ready for a nap after they graze. I feel a warm glow, a sense of peace."

"Your observations," Brother Shad smiled, "interpret well the artist's projected intention. Your interpretation of this end-time event of prophecy and the physical and emotional impact on society of this supernatural phenomenon should cause members of the church today to recognize the serenity of God's handiwork. The picture speaks of love, unity, care for each other, and the peace of God."

They moved in slow motion, step by step, toward his room until Melody stopped in front of another impressive picture. "Grandpa, do you see something special in this scene? The peace you mentioned about the lion and the lamb contrasted with this scene of Jesus asleep among His fearful disciples caused me to stop. They bob up and down on that small boat, tossed about by a tempestuous wind on the Sea of Galilee. What an ominous experience for the disciples."

"Tell me more of what you see in this picture," Grandpa Shad encouraged her power of observation.

"Evident to me, the fright on each face. I see bewilderment, unbelief, astonishment."

"Correct. Look again. What caused this predicament?"

"Grandpa, I think one can read part of the cause in the clouds painted by the artist. He implies a spiritual battle will soon erupt. I believe the artist portrays an attempted spiritual battle by Satan to swamp Jesus and His disciples, evidenced by the high winds and tumultuous waves. The enemy wanted to kill all of them."

"Right. But let's note the Bible passage description in Matthew 8:23-27. He awakens and then rebukes the wind. Jesus makes the entire occasion a lesson in faith for His group of twelve fearful, surprised, and shocked cabinet members. They learn to lean on Him and trust Him. It requires their total obedience to His lifestyle."

Tammy walked up behind the two while they conferred about the attributes and lessons learned from this last picture. She waited until their discussion concluded. Then, cleared her throat in order to announce her presence. "My watch and stomach tell me the dinner bell might clang any moment. May I invite you two to join me for dinner at the Fish 'n Steak House?"

"Yes, Mom. I'm famished."

"Did you say Fist 'n Skunk Horse? What is that?"

"No, Dad," Tammy spoke loud and slow, this time she looked directly at her dad. "We will eat dinner today at the Fish 'n Steak House. I came as soon as possible. I left the downtown church Sunday school class as soon as the teacher finished his presentation. His discussion continued, but the final prayer appeared nowhere in sight. So, I left."

The three family members continued their slow pace to the front door of the Center, because of Brother Shad's unsteady, but measured steps. Melody chatted non-stop and spoke in undertones to her mother: "Mom, Grandpa has developed a noticeable inability to hear. He dozed several times in the middle of Chaplain Sinclair's sermon. I had to squeeze his hand several times to keep him awake."

"Did he not sleep well last night?" Tammy whispered to Melody.

"No. He told me he experienced a bad dream, something about a terrible snowstorm when he grew up in his mid-teen years. Someone banged on their back door. But they saw no one when his dad opened the door. The dream bothered him all night. Because of the dream, he dozed in the chapel service. He said he did not sleep well last night. Mom," Melody asked quizzically, "why would Grandpa dream such a horrible thing?"

"Melody," Tammy turned sidewise to her daughter, "we need to pray for guidance for your grandfather. The Lord may desire to say something to him."

Tammy raised her voice and spoke loud and clear to her dad as they arrived at the front door of the Center. "Dad, please wait with Melody while I go drive the car up to the overhang area. The air seems cool. I shall return in a few minutes."

"Okay, my dear." The old man answered in obedience with a smile on his face. He knew a trip out for dinner would take him away from the mundane routine of the Center.

During the few minutes they waited for Tammy, Melody asked her grandfather: "Did anyone test your hearing within the last year?"

"No, never."

She held his hand, edged up close to his side, and met his eyes with hers. "Grandpa, I think it would help you interact better in conversations if you would allow Mom to take you for a hearing test. I believe you need to wear a hearing aid."

"No! I'm not deaf!" She grew fearful his blood pressure might go up, because his face reddened as he responded.

"Mom told me a few days ago your account includes sufficient money to buy a hearing aid."

"It would be too expensive. I don't want to spend the money, and I don't even know the amount in my checking account."

"I don't want to upset you, Grandpa. We want to have a nice Sunday afternoon dinner together. But will you pray about it, please? It will help you enjoy life and converse better with people."

"I suppose the vote stands at two to one?" He spoke slowly, holding his emotions in check.

"Yes." She buried her face in the old man's side and hugged him. He knew a pout would not change their decision.

Tammy parked under the canopy, sat in her car at the end of the sidewalk, and waited for her dad and daughter. *Why haven't they come out?* she pondered. *I can't honk the horn. It will disturb some of the residents . . . At last, here they come.*

"Dad, you sit in the front seat beside me. Then you can move in and out with ease."

Melody opened the door for the elder statesman, who backed in, dropped to the seat, and swung his legs, one at a time, into the car. The car ride gave him a sense of dignity. It perked up his attitude and perspective about the events of the day.

A few minutes earlier, he had felt like a delinquent juvenile, pressured by the hearing-aid discussion with Melody. But now, he sat up straight, eager for a ride off campus, filled with the expectation of a delicious meal in a good restaurant.

SUNDAY DINNER

"I like this vegetable stir-fry with the grilled chicken strips," Brother Shad said. "It satisfies my hunger, but the cook didn't give me enough grapes." The grapes enticed him to eat most of the veggies and pieces of chicken.

To show appreciation to Tammy for bringing him to dinner, he ate everything except for one-quarter of the rice that filled the bottom of his bowl-like plate. "I appreciate the regular brewed coffee, much better than the colored hot water served at the Center." He smacked his lips again and again as he savored every drop of his second cupful.

Family times of shared fellowship seldom happened these days because of Tammy's busy schedule at the city library as its director and Melody's school and church activities. With more involvement for them in these types of activities, Brother Shad often sat in his room and received fewer of their family visits.

Melody broke the peacefulness of the moment first and addressed her mother between mouthfuls of ice cream. "Mom, will you take Grandpa to a hearing specialist? He needs to wear hearing aids. I don't think he understands me, when I call him on the telephone."

"I agree. Telephone conversations with Dad test my patience. I think his inability to hear perplexes him, too."

"Dad, I want to come pick you up Tuesday afternoon and have your hearing examined."

"No! I'm not deaf! Just speak up, don't mumble. Then I can understand what you say."

"The situation involves all of us Dad. We desire pleasant times together like today. We want to build more forever-type memories." Tammy felt like a mother who must discipline her child.

"Is money available in my account for such an expenditure?"

"Yes, Dad. Your funds and your insurance coverage will last for several years."

"I don't want to do it," he protested. "But I will accept the fact you know what matters best for me."

"Dad, we love you and want quality time with you." Tammy chose her words carefully, not wanting to upset her dad. "Can you understand our desire, our predicament?"

"Yes, my dear. I don't want to, but I will agree to your decision."

"Thanks, Grandpa. This means you and I can spend more good times together. I won't shout and you need not frown when I come to see you."

With their tasty meal finished, the aged minister patted his two loved ones on their arms as they moved toward the car. "You two bring joy into my life. You make me happy when we come together. Let's please do this again soon."

"With your new hearing aid, Dad, it will open up a new vista of life for you and for us. Even though you will experience an adjustment period to the device, you will find restored relationships with people."

Melody held his arm tight when they approached the car. "Grandpa," She said with tears in her eyes, "You're my hero. I love you."

"Oh, my, my! You remind me of my beloved Katy. Then looking at his daughter with gratitude and appreciation for her kindness, he muttered with eyes half asleep: "Tammy, please take me home. I need rest and my afternoon nap after the enjoyment of our fellowship and such a delectable meal."

FAITH AND GOOD WORKS MAINTAINED
SATURDAY, NOVEMBER 3, 9:30 A.M.

Melody's telephone call conveyed good news to Brother Shad: "I will come visit you Saturday morning." It stirred his testosterone. He felt elated that his young granddaughter, now a Bible college freshman, would come and visit him, her aged grandfather.

He spoke out loud to himself, considering the complications of Melody's busy life. "She exudes energy and joy each time she interacts with me. I see exuberance and a certain carefree attitude that permeates her personality each time this young lady spends time with me.

"Our time together brings back warm memories of my beautiful helpmate Katy. I know after my demise the future will progress in good hands with young people like Melody who live a positive Christian lifestyle."

Melody arrived at the planned time and placed a rapid tap-tap-tap on his door. Courteous Melody waited for his invitation before greeting her grandpa "Good morning, May I come in?"

Brother Shad greeted her with a raised hand, then pointed to the chair beside his old lounge chair. "Please do come in. This chair has your name on it."

Melody gave her grandfather a big hug and loud smack of a kiss on his cheek. He felt glad he shaved earlier. "Grandpa, I left home early today in order to come through the snow. I could tell the plows worked long hours before dawn to clear that white stuff off the main roads."

"I can see it from my window when I look out at the fish pond. I estimate five inches of snow on the sidewalks."

Placing her coat across the back of the chair, she sat down and spoke with determination: "Grandpa, I need your help."

"How can an old man like myself be of any assistance to you?"

"I'm enrolled in an English composition class wherein each member must write a two-page essay."

"I know you well," he smiled broadly. "I think you will write a fine essay."

"I would like to write about you, Grandpa."

"Oh. Why about me?" His eyelids opened wide in disbelief.

"I would like to write about the adjustments you encountered throughout your seven years of living at the Center."

"You mean you want to write a ten-volume encyclopedia of how I sit in my chair day after day and wait for Jesus to come take me home?" He chuckled, not wanting to embarrass his granddaughter.

"No, Grandpa."

"I'm not a colorful, flamboyant movie actor. I'm just an old fossil, not quite petrified, but somewhat hardened," he affirmed. "My legs seemed less flexible this morning than when I stepped out of bed yesterday." He pointed to his shoes. "It was farther to the floor for my feet today than yesterday."

"Grandpa, please. I consider this essay assignment a serious endeavor. I admire your humor and I know it helped you endure and cope all these years in stressful situations, for sure at the Center."

"Okay. I will obey," he answered in a serious manner. "Just tell me what to say."

Melody leaned over to her grandfather, gave him another loud smack on his cheek and said, "Thank you, Grandpa. I knew I could count on you."

"Tell me again, please, what kind of information you desire." He began to look forward to the challenge of her request." With his hands cupping his head, he encouraged, "Help me set my mind in motion for your questions."

"First, how did you adjust to those people who passed by your doorway and interrupted your train of thought each day throughout these last seven years?"

"I found adjustment difficult when I arrived. I came in a stranger and felt alone. I soon found a different culture from the one back in my home state of South Dakota. Residents didn't trust me right away and I didn't trust them. To begin with, I didn't mix well and they didn't want to mix in social affairs with me.

"After a period of time, however, we began to trust each other. Their acceptance of me took time. I decided to make the most of this venue for my life." His hands, first clasped together, now began to accentuate his comments. "At last, they accepted me. I showed them respect. After time, we grew together like a family.

"The only person I knew here—Matti, thank God, came to see me each day. We knew each other back in 1954, over in the area where Katy and I began to pastor, before she married Dan. She assisted and helped me each day in the first weeks of my transition into the Center. Matti, a bookkeeper at one time, worked briefly for me in the district office.

"Later she helped transfer all my assets to the Center. Her selfless action required several meetings and telephone calls. She assisted me with patience through each step. The City Center Retirement Home provided my bed, my security, and three meals each day, my nursing care, and the services of a doctor.

"My responsibility to the Center—ask for assistance. They will take care of me until my death." Drawing a deep breath, he concluded, "I find the staff faithful to their word.

"Matti served me like a nanny. She called me on the telephone every day and came to see me every other day. We went for rides in the countryside, or off campus to buy a cup of coffee, or downtown to attend church. But now we attend chapel services at the Center.

"She helped me navigate through those different and difficult situations, like a walk on uneven sidewalks or ordering the best meal from a menu. These activities broke up my dull routine each day."

"So we call her Aunt Matti," Melody exclaimed, with a momentary pause in her writing in order to give her fingers a rest, "because she assisted you before Mom and I moved to town."

"Correct. You and Tammy came here to live four years later after I moved into the Center. When you came to town it meant so much to me. It raised my spirits. It made me happy and changed my loneliness to cheerfulness. I now know you exist but a telephone call away, like I might walk into a nearby room, sit down, and speak with you."

"Whenever I come to visit you, I see a few people tend to keep their doors closed." Her hands spoke like a ballerina in concert. "And I have observed few changes in decorations, in behavior, and activities of those residents."

"True. I keep my door open, because I want to build relationships with nearby residents and staff members. I try to share Jesus with the unsaved and encourage others with the Word, those who know the Lord. Few people in the Center express a working knowledge of the Bible.

"I read the Gospels three to four hours each day. Therefore, my mind remains filled with the Word of God. I feast on it throughout the day and after dinner in the evening. It helps me endure loneliness, the loss of family, and living in my sudden change-of-culture situation."

"Do the residents or staff converse with you," Melody inquired as she gazed into his eyes, "when you walk the corridors or eat with them in the dining room, attend chapel, or walk around the grounds?" Melody wanted clarification. She wasn't sure how much he said was wishful thinking or actual practice.

"I pray with people for a family member or for people to whom the Lord may lead me as I walk the corridors. I minister to others outside on my walks as I try to eradicate those infectious weeds, those pesky dandelions. But I try not to impose myself on anyone. I lift up Jesus and show people the steps to heaven. I encourage them. I like people and enjoy conversation.

"But this last year my activity diminished with the other residents. My memory continues to fail and confuses me." He scratched his head and blinked in confusion. "People come and go from here. I don't remember their names nor can I recall the events of these present days like the days of my first years here."

"Grandpa, did you ever experience any problem with physical or verbal abuse toward your person?" Melody wanted an in-depth interview with her grandpa. He obliged.

"No, Melody. From the time I came here, the staff and nurses ministered in helpfulness and kindness. The nurses treat me with utmost respect. People here associate with each other. I try to respond with sincere friendship.

"Oh yes, we must follow the rules. For instance, they schedule me for a shower each Tuesday and Saturday morning. I feel confident in their ability to take care of my needs—medical, physical ailments, food, personal items."

She continue to probe. "How does the staff react to your long periods of Bible study each day?"

"They don't bother me. They even encourage me in Bible study. It keeps my mind occupied each day. In fact, I read parts of different Bibles throughout the day. It helps me hold on to God's promises. I relax in the knowledge I can believe God each day to meet my need for whatever situation may arise.

"Some people at the Center watch TV most of the day." He wrinkled his nose. "To me, they seem to vegetate. What a sad way to live. I don't watch or listen to TV except for the Billy Graham reruns or an occasional TV preacher in the evening."

Melody's perceptions of retirement life at the Center turned from her grandfather's viewpoint to the thoughts and responses of other residents. She flipped through the pages of her notepad. "Grandpa, what do your associates in the nearby rooms think about each day as they sit in their rooms or as they congregate in the activities room? Do not some of them have active minds like yours?"

"I ask most people around me whether or not they love and serve Jesus. Most people in the Center love the Lord Jesus, which helps me to minister to them. When I walk down the corridors, people want to talk about their businesses, their jobs, their homes, their families. I try to direct them toward God's Word.

"But their minds do not make room for the Word of God like mine. Because I read the Word every day." He suddenly acted frustrated. "I want to share the Word with them. But they are not acquainted with it. It makes conversations rather one-sided and difficult."

"You never told me before, Grandpa, how you felt about your arrival at the Center nor what kind of emotional trauma you encountered. Of several difficult situations in your life, I see you as an over-comer, a survivor in your personal race to please Jesus. I consider myself a proud granddaughter, because I see you as one fine gentleman, a giant in the faith."

"I have said enough." His face turned red, "You embarrass me with those accolades. Go write your paper and don't fabricate anything in it about me. Tell the truth. Please don't add any incidents to it. Remember, Jesus looks over our shoulders at all times."

Then, standing, he exclaimed, "Give Him all glory and honor. I'm just one of His servants. John the Baptist said it well: 'I must decrease and He must increase' (John 3:30). Let's do our best to praise the Lord, not any of our own accomplishments."

Melody rose to leave, put on her coat, and felt she had succeeded in a superb interview. She gave her grandfather a hug, this time a long, noisy circular squeeze and two gentler kisses on his cheek. His cheeks turned pinkish, a big smile crossed his face.

A quick thought flashed through his mind. *She resembles her grandmother Katy. I'm blessed to receive such a large amount of time with my little cherub, now a gracious, resourceful woman. Yes, I'm most proud of her.*

Shad accompanied Melody to his open door. At his words of caution, she turned, their eyes met.

"Drive home with care, my love. Ice may cover the road."

"Yes Grandpa, I will drive with care. And, I shall entitle my essay: 'My Hero,' with the subtitle, 'A Man with a Passion for Souls.'"

The aged minister felt inspired as he returned to his chair by the window. But . . . *that young girl. Why did she visit me? She acted as though she knew me. Such a pleasant person. Lord, my memory has played tricks on me again.*

PART FOUR

WINTER: CHANGES THROUGH CRISES EVENTS

For I am persuaded that neither death nor life, nor angels nor principalities nor powers, nor things present nor things to come, nor height nor depth, nor any other created thing, shall be able to separate us from the love of God which is in Christ Jesus our Lord.
Romans 8:38, 39

CHAPTER TEN
SENILITY INTRUDES UNINVITED

Though I walk through the valley of the shadow of death, I will fear no evil, for You are with me.
Psalm 23:4

LIVING WITH INTEGRITY
MONDAY, NOVEMBER 5, 10:00 A.M.

"What will transpire in my schedule today?" Brother Shad wondered. "I should be prepared for visitors or interruptions. Who knows what may occur. I never know if new experiences my come my way and unfold during my day at the Center. I have shaved, put on a clean sport shirt, read ten chapters in the Book of John, and prayed for family and friends. I feel ready for visitors.

"But this recent winter storm may cause hostile landscapes and treacherous snow banks. Who might have the constitution to brave such blocked roads in order to come visit me today?

"I see a cardinal seated on a low branch outside my window. Ah, the Master Architect Himself, pieced together this beauty for my enjoyment this morning, carved in myriads of snow contours, untouched by human footprints."

The aged minister could hear the howling wind and see the changing sculptured scenes outside. The frost held geometric snowflakes tight to the frozen edges of his window. Thus, he felt encouraged to wear his favorite greenish-plaid knit sweater and heavy wool socks.

"Today I shall remain inside, stay warm, and read a book." For Brother Shad, that meant feasting on the remaining chapters of his projected reading schedule in the Book of John.

Settled in his worn lounge chair and involved in Bible reading, he remained oblivious to the nurses and attendants who passed by his open door. He kept his door open with the hope a visitor might appear.

This morning, Melody tapped on his door at the moment he completed his reading of chapter eleven. "Hi, Grandpa." Always exuberant in her greetings, she politely asked, "May I come in?"

"Hi yourself, my darling young one."

"Grandpa, don't you remember my name?" His face fell forward, his voice lowered in shame. Melody's face grimaced as she looked into her grandfather's blue eyes.

"Please tell me your name. My memory played tricks on me again."

"Grandpa, I'm Melody, Tammy's daughter." She slouched down in the chair near Brother Shad, exasperated.

"Melody dear, please forgive my bad memory." His eyes squinted, his composure unsettled. "What brings you out by yourself on a cold winter day to visit an old fossil like me?"

"We received a one-day vacation from our college classes, because of a major electrical outage on campus. Therefore, I felt today a good day to come visit." Her face beamed. "Also, I miss your company."

"You brightened my day too," he laughed. "I'm happy to see you."

"Grandpa, may I ask you a question? How did you develop character and integrity as you grew into manhood on the farm in Canada?"

"The influence of my dad, a very moral man, read a few chapters in his Bible each day. After dinner each evening we met in our living room. He conducted our family devotional time and pointed out specific Scripture passages to us by which to live and govern our lives. For example: *Trust in the LORD with all your heart. And lean not on your own understanding; In all your ways acknowledge Him, And He shall direct your paths*" (Proverbs 3:5, 6).

"Hold on just a moment. I want to write these thoughts in my journal. Okay, please continue."

"We learned and memorized this scripture. We savored it and we began to live its truth. It became a tenet of our daily life. And God did prove Himself. Let me tell you, the Lord provided rain at just the right time to break a drought and save our crops.

"We learned responsibility through the proper care of our animals, birds, and good management of the land. Each of the animals and domestic birds expressed different personalities. We learned to know their temperaments which helped us communicate with them. With 30 horses, 20 milk cows, 14 head of beef, 50 chickens, and 16 geese, plus two dogs and two cats, not to mention a spread of ten sections, patience was a necessity, endurance a given, wisdom most needful."

"How old were you, Grandpa, when you began to learn responsibility?"

"I don't know, except as the years went by we became aware of this kind of lifestyle to ensure survival. Dad instilled a love for the livestock in us children. When we worked the horses and gave them adequate rest periods, progress graced the workday.

"Also, the Lord provided abundant grass in the pasture lands so that the animals gave birth to healthy young ones. Through it all, we grew to appreciate the creative hand of the Lord in our family affairs, both at work and at play."

"What do you mean, Grandpa?"

"Our family became a team, I think a better team than our high school baseball gang. As we grew up, my siblings found their strengths in working around the farm or in household duties. We worked through differences of opinion and learned over time to pull together in our individual and group assignments.

"Dad excelled as an administrator and spiritual head for our family. He found work for all of us to do each day. But he allowed time for rest and play."

Melody listened wide-eyed and attentive. She had never heard any explanations before of this aspect of his upbringing. "You told me you played on a community baseball team. Can you tell me your batting average?"

"I don't know. I remember I developed the ability to hit the ball most times and score a couple of runs for each of our games." He spoke with increased excitement. "But, I loved the farm work more than the game of baseball, until an evangelist came to our church. At one of his meetings, I gave my life to Jesus."

"What effect did your mom have on your growing up years?" Melody knew enough about interviewing not to ask him a "yes" or "no" type question.

"Melody, she worked hard, excelled as a fine cook, made clothes for us, and gave each youngster individual attention. She did not talk fast, but conversed with each of us in practical ways." With palms together, he glanced over her shoulder, as if seeing the scene he remembered.

"Like Dad, she made a point in each of her conversations with us. Our talks never lasted long. But her love for each of us showed through the activity of the day. We knew it by the scarves and gloves she knitted for us and the generous amount of food she served at meals.

"Even though we did not have a fancy home and did not have several things you might observe in the home of a well-to-do family, Mom made our house a warm home by her loving care for each of us. She demonstrated a need to touch us. We children received lots of hugs."

"I can see, Grandpa, how you learned character through your growing-up years. Did your brothers and sisters learn character in a similar manner?"

"No, not all. My oldest brother, 15 years my senior, hated the farm life, its daily disciplines, and isolated social restrictions. I suppose because of his attitude, Dad Milburn eventually gave oversight of the farm to me. I found the challenges connected with farm life a fine way to utilize a variety of skills—arithmetic, accounting, marketing, and so on."

Melody perceived he enjoyed being interviewed, recalling youthful memories of his childhood. "Grandpa, how did you learn the difference between character and integrity?"

"I learned integrity by not eating all the homemade oatmeal cookies Mom placed on a plate at the end of the kitchen counter." He hung his head in shame, remembering the incident.

"She set out those pastries for all of us kids to share and enjoy at snack time. Integrity concerns more than honesty. I learned not to steal my brothers' and sisters' rights to their portion of those goodies.

At that point, I gained their respect, and my character began to improve." With one eye closed, the other remaining open, he smacked his lips as if remembering the taste of those mouthwatering oat meal cookies.

"I think I turned seven the day Dad sat me down on a kitchen stool and talked with sternness about the *cookies-on-the-counter* principles of life, of people's needs, and the importance of service to others. This discussion concerned my character and the lack of it.

"Over the next few years, I found out that integrity grows from within and describes the inner you. Like an oak tree, it takes a lifetime to build. Proverbs 11:3 states these thoughts in clear terms: 'The integrity of the upright will guide them.'"

"I surely don't see much of that quality in my class mates."

"Melody, character shows the imprint in your life, of your moral qualities and ethical standards. It highlights your temperament and disposition, how you actively conduct yourself among people.

"Integrity develops in a person's life by performing law abiding, virtuous, fair-minded, honorable, genuine, truthful and honest actions. Thus, a person with integrity desires to do right in each situation of his or her private and public life."

"I like your insights, Grandpa. Integrity describes the real me and my character shows how I interact and relate to other people."

"Believe it. Practice it. Live it. Then the Lord can bless you," he concluded as she grasped the importance of their discussion.

"Grandpa, several of my classmates pooh-pooh honesty. They do whatever they can to pass a test or appear to achieve success. For myself, I want Jesus as my senior partner, my constant guide and helper."

"Melody, I see that lack of reliance on Jesus here at the Center. Not everyone lives a life dedicated to responsibility. Some attendants seem more interested in clocking-in forty hours per week than in the provision of quality assistance and health care. Some residents don't keep their rooms tidy. Some visitors disturb residents by their boisterous lifestyles. Some television sets blare all the time which makes conversation an impracticality."

"How do you cope, Grandpa?" She acted dismayed at his responses.

"I try to see the best in every person and treat them with dignity and respect. People respond to kindness." He leaned forward, touched her arm, and continued as he looked straight at her face. "I don't look for a fight.

"Trust builds up a person. It gives him something to hold on to and to believe for the future. Certain residents here need positive prayer, a smile of encouragement, a bit of help, and a sympathetic listener."

"Does life here stress you, Grandpa?" she asked, holding his hand, a look of concern on her face.

"Yes, my dear. It changed the way I minister to people. I now live *among* my congregation. Before I came to the City Center, I could retreat into my home on occasion for spiritual and physical renewal. But not here. I must lose myself in Jesus, while I sit in my lounge chair, regardless of the noise in the hall or visitors who pass by.

"My life became regulated by the routine of the Center. In one way, I reside like a pawn on a chessboard," he added, mouth twisted. "I must do what I'm told. I enjoy little freedom except when someone comes to take me off campus.

"But no one can take away my spiritual life. To keep it, I pray and read my Bible. The Lord sustains me," he said happily, pointing upward. "I know He lives in me, guides me, and I feel His presence at all times."

Knock, knock.

"Look who came to see me today." Shad arose, walked toward the door, and motioned, "Come in, Matti."

"Hi, Aunt Matti. Grandpa Shad told me stories of how he grew up in Canada and learned integrity and character on the farm."

"Integrity, yes; character? Well, the Lord may keep him in boot camp for a while, yet."

"Matti," Shad pursed his lips and sat down. "I want Melody to see my best side. Don't lecture me about character. The Holy Spirit grinds on me and continues to polish me, even in these last twenty-four hours. I'm not yet sanctified. For example, they served our meal forty-five minutes late last night. I declare, that happens perhaps once every ten days.

"Do you know what they served? Hot dogs." His cheeks turned pink; his throat muscles twitched. "I do not like hot dogs. No one becomes fat on the food they serve from this kitchen."

His face wrinkled; his eyes squinted; his nose flared; his color changed to hot red. "I even waited thirty minutes for a cup of coffee." He clicked his gums and ground his teeth. "And guess what? It arrived cold."

"Brother Shad, why don't the three of us go to the Pizza House for lunch? They serve a nice buffet you have enjoyed on previous trips. The coffee comes hot." Aunt Matti spoke in a gentle way, using her knack in communication with people to smooth out his ruffled feelings.

"Melody, might you take time to eat lunch today with a cantankerous old man?" the subdued resident responded.

"I would consider it an honor, Grandpa, to put my feet under the same table with a fine gentleman like yourself." Melody in quick order had learned from Aunt Matti the virtues of smooth interpersonal relationships.

Is that integrity or is that a display of character? Aunt Matti smiled as the three exited the room. They walked arm in arm down the corridor and basked together in God's embrace. *Our pizza shall taste extra special today.* Matti intuitively knew today's activities signified a good day for Brother Shad.

PHYSICAL AILMENTS INCREASE
MONDAY, NOVEMBER 12, 7:30 A.M.

TE-da-la-DAAT-RING, ring.

She knew from her cell phone ring who would call her at this hour, Brother Shad with another problem. Aunt Matti became the first person to hear of each situation. He called her at this hour whenever upset, sick, or when he needed assistance.

She reached for the phone, while yet in bed, eyelids half open. With calmness she said, "Brother Shad, did you sleep well last night?"

"No, Matti. My back aches, my leg muscles continue to cramp, my right hand shakes. I can't get out of bed. My head feels tight when I try to put my feet down over the edge of my bed. When I do that much, I start to feel dizzy. Matti, do you think the end has started for me?"

"Did the aide bring your breakfast this morning?"

"Yes, it arrived about three minutes ago."

"Did you eat anything yet?"

"No."

"What kind of fruit or juice sets on your tray?"

"I think, orange juice. I can't see with clarity. Everything looks fuzzy."

"Brother Shad, are you sitting up on the edge of your bed?"

"Yes."

"Try to drink your orange juice. Do it slowly. Don't tilt your head back fast. Afterward, lie down again. I will come see you about 10 a.m. In the meantime, I will pray for you. In fact, let me pray now."

"Yes. Please pray for me, Matti."

"Father God, Brother Shad does not feel well this morning. Will You please touch him with Your healing presence."

"Yes, Lord. Thank You, Lord."

"Minister your physical help to Brother Shad's eyes, his head, his back, and legs."

"Oh, thank You, Lord Jesus."

"Satan, stop your harassment of Brother Shad. The blood of Jesus covers him. Take your demons of sickness and leave. I rebuke and bind you in the name of Jesus."

"Yes, Lord, I agree. Let it be done in Jesus' name."

"We agree together, Lord. Thank You for Your presence and Your touch to heal Brother Shad. Amen. Brother Shad, can you see your food plate now?"

"Yes, the dizziness left me. I see orange juice on my tray."

"Drink your juice and eat what makes you feel comfortable."

"Okay, Matti."

"Then lie down and rest. I'll come and see you at 10 a.m." She knew Brother Shad often needed a person to talk to, a voice to hear his ailments.

"God bless you, my friend." Ever appreciative, he tried to present himself the picture of a gentleman.

MATTI'S SNOOZE INTERRUPTED

Aunt Matti stretched out in her cozy bed after they concluded their conversation and closed her eyes to relax. Within three breaths she fell asleep. The night before she completed her evening schedule of financial book work, letters to friends, e-mail messages, leisure reading, with lights turned off at 2:00 a.m. Deep sleep engulfed her body.

With a sudden jolt, her eyes burst wide open at 8:52 a.m. "Oh! Lord, help me get myself together. Do I hear rain on the window? Yes." She arose from her warm bed, dressed, and remembered her promise to Brother Shad. "Let me see, how does this orange skirt look with my tan blouse? No. I can't wear open-toed shoes today."

"Because of this rain, a cool day," she told herself. With another look through her wardrobe, "I shall wear my black strap, medium-height shoes, and a reddish-brown wool skirt with matching long-sleeved light brown blouse adorned with a few sequins at the neckline. My long-sleeved, light-green wool vest with two small pockets for Kleenex will keep me warm."

Her breakfast consisted of one hard-boiled egg, a glass of grape juice, one slice of toasted Ezekiel bread spread with a thin coat of almond butter. She brewed her usual cup of regular coffee, no sugar, no cream. A glass of water enabled her to swallow several supplements: among them, a vitamin C, an acidophilus, and a multivitamin.

"Let me see, which clock has the correct time?" A glance at her watch indicated 9:40 a.m. "Okay, I'm ready for the day's care-giving activities, first with Brother Shad." She adjusted her coat, opened the kitchen door, and prepared to enter the garage, but an incoming call on her cell phone interrupted her plans.

I think I shall let it ring, she decided. *No, I will answer. Any number of persons may call.*

"Hello. May Jesus reign supreme." Aunt Matti answered in her best, cheery response.

"Matti, Sandra Ridenhorst here. Sid and I will come to town for supplies tomorrow. How about lunch together at the Fish 'n Steak House tomorrow noon? And would you like to bring Brother Shad, too?"

"Let me talk with him. I expect to see him soon. I think he might come. He enjoys company. Few people stop to see him anymore. He appreciates the opportunity to eat out."

"Good. See you tomorrow noon."

"Bye, Sandra."

She prepared to exit her garage, but a distant scene of a Sunday evening service flashed through Aunt Matti's mind. She recalled Brother Shad had delivered a two-part evangelism series, entitled "The Glory of God," for both the a.m. and p.m. services twenty-four years ago in Dan and Aunt Matti's church. As a result, several persons came to the altar and dedicated their lives to the Lord.

She sat in her car, eyes wide open, her mind mesmerized on the notable events of that day. The memory of the series triggered a return in her mind to the worship CD she had played minutes earlier during breakfast. Her husband Dan sang: *Is It Any Wonder?* The words stood out in her consciousness, which made concentration on other tasks difficult. Before she turned on the ignition key, Dan's voice resounded in her mind again.

His rendition of those lush melodies captivated her attention. The reality of Dan's effortless vocal abilities brought back musical moments to Aunt Matti. Out loud she acknowledged: "Dan, I miss you. I miss our music ministry. I miss—oh, I know. I still grieve over the fact you left me ten years ago and now live with Jesus. Life alone without you—I don't like it."

She backed out of the garage in a hurry and wasted no time as she maneuvered through traffic in order to keep her scheduled appointment with Brother Shad.

AN UNEXPECTED VISITOR

The click-clomp of cold weather shoes in the corridor alerted the sleepy Brother Shad of Aunt Matti's approach. She walked with purpose in her stride. The habit began early in her life when her mother delivered a baby brother born at Matti's age of 17 years. Soon after his birth, her mother became diagnosed with terminal lung cancer.

Aunt Matti assumed her mother's duties by default for all of his growing up years. On occasion, the situation embarrassed her.

Pastors who visited her father's home believed she had conceived the baby out of wedlock.

"Matti, I drank the orange juice on my breakfast tray, but ate no food. When I open my eyes, my head feels like it could spin like a top. I can't focus my eyes. Things move when I open my eyes, my head aches." Brother Shad knew Aunt Matti stood beside his bed because he recognized her perfume, a faint aroma of Jovan Island Gardenia.

She placed her hand on his forehead. "You don't have a temperature. Your forehead feels warm, but not hot."

"Will this begin the end for me?" he asked a second time as he looked up at her with blurred vision.

"I don't think so. I called Tammy a few minutes ago on my way here. She told Melody. We prayed for you and will continue to do so. I also asked Chaplain Sinclair to place your name on his prayer list and to alert the City Center prayer chain for you.

"Let me lay my hand on your arm and stand beside you for a while. May I pray for you again?"

"Please, Matti." Brother Shad acted restless. Forced to lie down, he manifested just enough energy to groan.

"Dear Lord, You know all about this physical condition of Brother Shad. We ask You to give him relief in all parts of his body. Clear his mind, relax his body, relieve the tension in his head, comfort him, heal his eyes, stop the ringing in his ears. Father, I pray You place Your powerful healing touch on my friend. Thank You, Jesus. Amen."

"Matti, I see a person behind you. He stands near your shoulder, seems focused on me."

She looked behind herself, confused, "I don't see anyone in your room."

"Such a tall man. What does he want?"

She looked around again, her eyes searching all corners of the room, "Do you still see him?"

"Yes. He placed his hands on my legs. My ankles—oh, hot. Matti, my legs tingle with heat."

"I feel it, too. Something radiated down my right side. From my shoulder to my foot, it felt like a vibrating pad touched my whole right side." Matti looked down to examine herself. She regained her self-control and began to breathe with regularity once again.

"My body feels better," Brother Shad exclaimed, "my back doesn't ache and my head doesn't feel tight. Did you hear him? As he turned to leave, he told me he would come again."

"What does it mean?" Aunt Matti questioned, as she looked toward the door again. "When will he come?"

"I don't know. I guess he went out the door. I don't know how he left us. Matti, do you think he will come again, perhaps take me to Jesus?"

CHAPTER ELEVEN

SPECIAL VISITORS MINISTER

*I sought the LORD, and He heard me,
And delivered me from all my fears.*
Psalm 34:4

FRUSTRATION IN SOCIAL ENCOUNTERS
MONDAY, NOVEMBER 12, 3:30 P.M.

AUNT MATTI FOLLOWED HER HABIT of appearing mid-afternoon after his nap. "I went earlier to see my three friends before I came to tell you that Sandra and Sid Ridenhorst extended an invitation for us to join them for lunch tomorrow noon at the Fish 'n Fries Steak House."

She sat in the chair beside Brother Shad's and felt a consultation with him a possible option, now that he had recuperated from his morning ailments.

Earlier he lay relaxed and fell asleep soon after the mid-morning visitation of both Aunt Matti and his unknown visitor. It enabled his daily routine to resume in time for lunch with his two buddies, Phillip and Henry, followed by his one-hour afternoon nap. "Do you feel well enough you might consider a lunch to include grapes and melon at the Steak House tomorrow noon with Sandra and Sid?"

"Well, I like that possibility."

"I think it a good opportunity for you to enjoy a change of scenery and eat different food."

"Do you recommend this excursion?" He closed his Bible to consider the request and laid it on his book table.

"Yes. You will enjoy fellowship with the Ridenhorsts and good food offered by a fine menu."

Ever cautious because of his memory problems, he expressed doubt. "Do I know these people?"

"Yes, we interacted in ministry together thirty years ago in South Dakota. When we talk together at lunch, you may recall some of the times you spoke in those camp meetings in the Black Hills."

"I feel embarrassed and ashamed to tag along. I do not remember people's names and events about which you speak. I would enjoy the outing and the food, but my conversational ability remains limited, because my memory fails me."

His hands covered his face. "I might act as a burden. I don't think I should put them through the torture of my inability to remember them or our relationship in ministry. I would grope like a foreigner, unable to speak the language."

"Will you go with me? I think it most appropriate for you to come eat with us." Matti realized she needed to exercise her best persuasive arguments.

"No," he said, looking out the window to avoid her persistence.

"They serve good food," she spoke softly.

"My memory plays tricks on me. I can't converse well. I might lie when he asked me, 'How could I live with that guilt?' I could not. No. I would rather drink lukewarm coffee here and read my Bible."

He squirmed, "My real comfort comes at the time I read God's Word. It helps prepare me to meet my Jesus." Placing a hand on his Bible, he declared, "Jesus talks to me through His Word."

The two old friends spoke to each other with frankness. The exchange about lunch with the Ridenhorsts opened Aunt Matti's eyes to Brother Shad's current mental perceptions and continued physical deterioration. Even though he spoke with clarity, albeit slowly, she sensed a new level in his lowered cognitive abilities not observable weeks earlier.

Aunt Matti felt her colleague, often bold and demonstrative, had entered into a new phase of narrowed interest in people and social events at the Center. It cause consternation in her dialogue with him. *He seems withdrawn or do I just imagine a change?*

When Aunt Matti left Brother Shad that afternoon, her intuition told her other mental changes may soon occur. She commented as she prepared to leave his room, "I shall enjoy lunch with the Ridenhorsts, but lunch will taste flat without your presence."

The light rain continued as Brother Shad walked Aunt Matti to the front door, then lumbered back to his lounge chair. *Thank you, Tammy, for the cushion you brought and placed over my broken lounge chair seat. It serves two purposes. I can see out my window from a higher point and I can aim and drop in order to sit in this temporary renovation of my favorite piece of furniture.*

At this moment, his thought processes cleared and ran full speed ahead. *What a soggy day. A day for inside activity; not a day to attempt a walk outside. Those pesky dandelions—good riddance, dead for this season. If Jesus hasn't come for me by next spring, I shall start earlier with a spade and a three-gallon bucket to slaughter those proliferating, yellow crowned obnoxious weeds.*

His smile, became a disguised snarl. "I don't think I shall see dandelions in heaven. At least, I hope not."

He adjusted the extra chair cushion, settled back, stroked his chin, and reminisced: *Ridenhorst . . . Ridenhorst. I recall the name of a farm family who lived ten miles northwest of us when I grew up.*

Ridenhorst, yes, their son Joseph played second base on our high school baseball team, good slugger, too.

His disgust turned into a broad smile. *He might be the father of Sid Ridenhorst. Perhaps I should call Matti and invite myself to lunch tomorrow. We might talk about something of interest tomorrow after all.*

Before he walked to supper, he telephoned Matti. "Brother Shad here. Count me in for lunch tomorrow." Excited, his voice sounded upbeat. "I changed my mind. I'll tell you why when you pick me up."

SLUGGER JOSEPH RIDENHORST

After supper, he cleaned his dentures, returned to his lounge chair by the window, and intended to write a letter, but his mind remained stayed on Joseph his young high school friend. *I remember Joseph. Dad would send Aaron and me over to the Ridenhorst farm each year in early December to buy a pine tree for our Christmas celebration. Joseph, one year behind me in school, 16 years old, a good athlete, played baritone horn in band.*

Hmm. . . . Yes, I remember. He gave his life to the Lord one month after me at the revival in our hometown. I often wondered what happened to Joseph, a good friend and cheerful classmate. Sid might tell me more about Joseph tomorrow at lunch.

This long-forgotten remembrance brought other scenes to Brother Shad's mind of activities and acquaintances during his teenage years. The most vivid reflection, a Christmas when Shad turned twelve. Aaron, Michelle and he drove to the Ridenhorst farm to purchase a seven-foot evergreen tree. "You may take the tree," Mr. Ridenhorst stated, "for the cost of one live goose and two live chickens."

With care they laid it in the bed of the family 1927 Chevrolet truck. The date: Saturday morning, the twelfth of December. Michelle drove home with care in order to avoid snow banks and potholes. All three teenagers beamed with joyous spirits and sang Christmas carols on their return. Michelle began with *Angels We Have Heard on High*; the three followed with their rendition of *O Come All Ye Faithful*.

The weather turned frigid on their return, a Canadian clipper passed over them. "I feel too cold to sing," Aaron chattered.

Upon their arrival home, Mom Bertha Milburn served lunch and hot chocolate. Dad Horatio Milburn said: "Everyone must eat lunch before we trim the tree and decorate the house."

The entire family sensed the spirit of Christmas, even their pet skunk, Snipe, now eight weeks old. Snipe and Aaron had developed an affinity for each other. Aaron even allowed Snipe to sleep on his bed at night.

The Milburn clan, a happy close-knit family, lived with the older children taught to protect, assist, and guide their younger siblings. When Jesus came into their lives during the revival in Weyburn one year earlier, attitudes of "mine, mine" diminished. Older family members realized the rough edges in their part of the family relationships also needed a tune up and overhaul.

Brother Shad's Dandelions

"Dad, may we place the tree in the middle of the living room this year rather than by the front window?" Michelle pleaded. "Then, we can see all sides of the tree and the decorations on it."

"Sounds good to me. What do you think, Mom?" A careful manager of finances, Dad Milburn acted like a diplomat. His intuition told him to stay out of certain areas of discussion or debate, with one of those activities—the placement of Christmas decorations in the house.

"Okay, if everyone will help," she said, wiping her hands on a kitchen towel.

"What shall we do first, Mom?" shouted Aaron.

Shad, in almost the same breath, asked: "Mom, where do we begin?" Both boys expressed excitement with Christmas now a tangible reality.

Michelle squared off a space in the center of the living room with hand motions. "Our new tree will look beautiful right here."

"Boys, go build a two-foot square box in which we shall place the tree," instructed Mom Milburn. "Place a bottom on the box into which we can nail the bottom of the tree. Nail it in with cross boards and fill the box with several rocks for weight. We don't want the tree to fall over.

"After we secure the tree and it stands upright, let's drape an old sheet over the rocks and box to make it look like snow." She organized details well. "Then, we can string popcorn around the tree and hang some tinsel on the branches.

"Everyone to their jobs. Michelle, you and I shall decorate the living room while the men go build the tree box." Mom Milburn exuded excitement like the teenagers over the decoration plans for Christmas, her favorite season of the year.

By mid-afternoon the finished box with the secured tree in it, looked like it belonged in the living room. Fist-size rocks placed around the tree gave it stability. The tree looked elegant, ready for eager hands to decorate its outstretched arms.

Dad Milburn cautioned, "I will supervise the placement on certain branches of our clip-on candle holders. We want to prevent any danger of a fire hazard. Remember the rule for these finger-length candles: two hours maximum allowed for lighted time.

CONGENIAL NURSE HOTCHKISS

"Brother Shad . . . Brother Shad," Nurse Hotchkiss entered his door and interrupted the spell of his reflections of his classmate Joseph and of a tree-trimming event decades earlier. "I came to give you your pill and evening snack."

"Thank you, young lady. I dreamed about a Christmas years ago up in Canada. I turned twelve that year. Did you ever bring a live tree into your home for Christmas when you grew up?"

"Yes, in Walhalla, North Dakota. We would buy a pine tree from a farm friend who owned land by the river. My two brothers went with our dad to cut it down. The men traveled on a bobsled to find a satisfactory tree. My sister and I trimmed the tree after the guys secured it in the corner of our living room.

"Those were special days. While they scouted for a tree, they had to keep a watchful eye out for moose. Moose can be dangerous. They browsed and bedded down in the same area where we harvested our Christmas trees."

When Nurse Hotchkiss exited to continue her night rounds, Brother Shad resumed his day-dream about Christmas. *I wished the season prompted more people to think about Jesus, and the reason why He came to earth.*

He began his preparations for bed. *Christmas time brings joy. But who did I recall before Nurse Hotchkiss came into my room? I'm tired. Maybe tomorrow I'll remember something about — John? Joseph? Who? Anyway, I hope Tammy will come tomorrow and take me out for lunch.*

ANGELIC HELPERS ON ASSIGNMENT
TUESDAY, NOVEMBER 13, 7:30 A.M.

"Tall Man came again last night, Matti," Brother Shad spoke into his telephone receiver with animation. "Big Guy stood at his side as Tall Man talked to me. He cupped his hands, cradled my head in his large, smooth hands, and told me: 'I will not take you to Jesus, yet. He needs you here. Continue your ministry. I shall come for you in the appropriate season.'"

"Matti, the power of God flowed through his hands. It helped me sleep well last night. My headache cleared; no aches, no jabs pounded my forehead and ears. Matti, what can this mean? At what ministry shall I continue? I don't know how or to whom.

"They departed right after they spoke to me. And I know, they visited me." Brother Shad's call to Aunt Matti conveyed enthusiasm she had not witnessed in recent conversations with the old man.

"Their presence emphasizes the Lord loves you," Aunt Matti responded.

"I do wish they would take me home soon to Jesus." Matti had to hold the receiver slightly away from her ear because of his bombastic enthusiasm.

"It will happen at the right time, my friend. God will make it clear to you in His own schedule. For now, consider how you might pray for Tammy, Melody, and me. And don't forget to pray for each person in the rooms around you. Also, include our pastors, missionaries, Bible school personnel, and students in your devotional moments. "I wonder if the Lord did not yet designate a satisfactory replacement for your ministry. He might prepare you for a special ministry in heaven. Have you thought of that possibility? What does the Lord want to teach you, Brother Shad, or perfect here in your life on earth?"

"Oh, I feel tired, Matti. He can take me just as I am. My salvation has no basis in my accomplishments or my work or my desires."

"True, but what might the Lord do for the lack of patience in your daily routine?"

"Matti, you sound like an attorney prepared to cross-examine me. I lived guilty of sin before Jesus came into my life. He forgave my sins, gave me His free gift of salvation, and has covered me by His blood atonement.

"I grant you one thing though: I pray for more fruit of the Holy Spirit in my life every day." His verbal reply changed from a condescending attitude to one like the administrator he had expressed earlier in his life.

"I don't think I'll ever have enough love, joy, and peace, not even self-control (Galatians 5:22, 23) in my activities with the staff and my visitors. Smooth interpersonal relationships with people remain important to me. Matti, we all need good smooth interactions with the attendants and staff in the Center, even with the board members when they make their own informal inspections of the rooms.

"Some of these staff personnel and residents express great personal needs to me. I try in indirect ways to bring joy into their lives—like a smile coupled with a cheerful greeting. I want to encourage each person whenever I can."

He lowered his head slightly and looked over the top of his glasses. "In all these interactions, I try to add value to their lives. I want to leave them with a feeling of their having received a blessing from the Lord."

"Your thoughts are well spoken, Brother Shad. Remember, today we shall have lunch with Sid and Sandra Ridenhorst. I will come and pick you up at 10:45 a.m. Please be sure to shave and put on a clean sport shirt." She spoke slowly to encourage him. "One of your western string ties would look nice with it in case they might want to take pictures."

"Okay, Matti. I will remember and make myself ready by 10:45 a.m."

AT THE FISH 'N STEAK HOUSE

Brother Shad and Aunt Matti arrived at the Fish 'n Fries Steak House at 11:45 a.m. as planned. Aunt Matti's intuition, however, told her something appeared wrong. She felt uneasy about the walk into the restaurant. "Brother Shad, let's sit here a moment. I need to pray about the restaurant. 'Lord, You know this situation? What happened? I feel hesitant. Why?'"

Whee-dah! whee-dah!

The strident blare of a nearby ambulance siren sounded urgent. The large white vehicle with flashes of intense red lights approached the driveway to their right. It screeched to a halt one car width away from Matti's front bumper.

Matti and Brother Shad sat in stunned silence and watched the drama unfold as one waiter held the restaurant doors open while two ambulance attendants vanished inside with a gurney.

"What happened in the restaurant?" Brother Shad questioned, eyes wide open in amazement.

"I have a premonition, a bad feeling in my stomach," Aunt Matti replied, as she shielded her eyes from the glare of the bright ambulance lights. Before either could utter another comment, the attendants wheeled out their stretcher with the body of a man strapped in. Sandra walked close behind, trying her best to holdback a flow of tears.

Sandra and Aunt Matti's eyes met as the EMTs pushed the cot into the ambulance. Before she climbed into the back of the ambulance, Sandra spoke through her tears: "Sid experienced another heart attack as we entered the restaurant. They think he's dead. No pulse."

The entire scenario transpired in less than three minutes. As the ambulance sped away, Matti spoke first: "We must eat somewhere else. I couldn't bear to go inside this restaurant today. Do you have a suggestion?"

"No. I agree. You choose." Brother Shad groaned in sympathy and shook his head in dismay.

"Shall we go to the Pizza and Pickle Jar? They have a noon buffet. We could enjoy a variety of vegetables and pizza followed with a dish of ice cream."

"I shall accompany you there with pleasure, provided they make hot coffee."

"After we eat, I shall take you back to the Center. Then I must check with Sandra at the hospital to see about Sid's condition." In minutes they were seated and ready to order. "What kind of pizza would satisfy your appetite?" Matti inquired.

"I like every kind, most of all chicken, cheese, and veggies. Whatever you choose, I will eat. Please order for me. Tell the waitress I want a "hot" cup of coffee."

Part way through their meal, Aunt Matti's cell phone rang.

"Matti, Sandra here. Sid died in the ambulance, cardiac arrest. I wanted you to know first since we planned lunch together today. Please excuse me now. I must contact our families."

Aunt Matti wondered: *Sandra spoke with haste, seldom took a breath, still in shock. I heard no tears. Oh, my dear friend. I shall call her this evening. She needs someone with whom to talk.*

"Finished yet, Brother Shad? I feel filled up. I enjoy your company, but this event makes it difficult to swallow a meal. What a sad situation. Shall we go?"

"Yes, Matti. I finished my coffee. I, too, feel disappointed and shaken. I expected to engage Sid in a good conversation about his dad. I think his dad, Joseph, became one of my high school friends. This type of lost activity and excitement raises my blood pressure. Please take me home."

THE UPSET BIRDIES

Brother Shad awakened at 3 p.m., groggy from his siesta. He washed his face which cleared his mind. "First, I shall eat the orange slices left for me this morning by my young pastor friend, Brother Carpenter. Then a walk around the corridor, maybe three times, will strengthen my legs and improve my circulation."

"Brother Shad, time for your afternoon pill and shake." Nurse Hotchkiss smiled as she entered his room, handed him the medicine, and exited. On her way out, he heard her hum a line of *It Is Joy Unspeakable*.

"Why, bless my soul. Do I see the same Nurse Hotchkiss? I believe something nice has happened to her. 'Lord, bless this dedicated nurse. I thank You she places my welfare uppermost in her actions. Please keep Your hand of protection upon her.'"

After downing his pill and shake, he rose from his chair and began his mid-afternoon walk of the corridors. Near his door sat an 83-year-old lady: "Hi Thelma, did you receive a driver's license yet for your new wheelchair?"

"No, Brother Shad. They said I look too young to drive. But look, this chair came fitted for a left-foot drive. I wanted a right-foot drive with an automatic gear shift." Thelma gave quick replies whenever Brother Shad teased her.

A widow of thirteen years, she had arrived at the Center two years earlier. Her family of three sons and ten grandchildren visited each week. Thelma occupied a room two doors away from Brother Shad. When certain loud members of her family visited, he would hear their laughter.

Next, the aged minister walked past the door of Helen's Beauty Shop. She looked up, smiled, and said: "Good afternoon, Brother Shad. How about a haircut today?"

"That time again? I don't feel any hair on my ears yet," he said moving both hands to his head. "When that happens, it's like flies buzz around my head. I'll come in a few days, Helen."

A nearby attendant counseled as he continued his walk: "Don't stumble here, sir. I just cleaned and mopped the floor from this spot down to the activities room. Your neighbor, Agnes, had a problem. Her lunch didn't set well today. As a result, her walker slipped out from her grasp. She fell and bruised her elbow in the middle of the remains of her lunch. Fortunately, no broken bones."

"Thank you, Jimmy. I shall watch every step. God bless you."

Brother Shad continued his walk toward the receptionist's desk. "Hello, Mrs. Penderholt. Are the birds happy with their songs today?"

"I think those little birds seem upset. Brother Shad, they flitter from branch to branch in their big glass cage. I went over to see if I might find anything unusual. They have food and water. Maybe the outside weather affects them. I heard on the Weather Channel this morning there could be a snowstorm coming our way tomorrow. Perhaps the drop in temperature and air pressure upset them."

"I will go stand by their cage and offer a prayer to calm them down. You know, the Lord of all creation, of all birds, animals, fish, and mankind, sees their dilemma." He glanced over the birds as he slowly walked to the cage.

"Little friends, don't be worried. Our Heavenly Father knows your need. His hand supports you; His love surrounds you; His angels guard you." Brother Shad spoke to the birds with compassion as if they were a part of his early-life farm flocks.

"'Lord Jesus, please quiet down our little friends; settle them in their routine each day. Console them as You have comforted me many times in my life. In Jesus' name, I pray. Amen.'"

"Look, Brother Shad, your prayer worked. Our little songsters started to serenade each other again. What beautiful melodies."

"Let's give all the glory to God, Mrs. Penderholt. 'Thank You again, Jesus.' Our Heavenly Father knows all our needs, even those of our gorgeous little feathered companions."

As he walked back down the hall toward his room, Brother Shad thought: *Well, Matti, it looks like my ministry includes prayers for our petite, feathered friends.*

CHAPTER TWELVE

SALVATION SETTLES DESTINY

*Be ready, for the Son of Man is coming
at an hour you do not expect.*
Matthew 24:44

A CHANGE OF ADDRESS EXPECTED
WEDNESDAY, NOVEMBER 14, 10:00 A.M.

THE TWO MINISTERIAL FRIENDS – caregiver and care receiver, sat in Brother Shad's room and began to reminisce about the paths their lives had traveled. The aged pastor recalled "I once learned a poem in high school that describes my life, *The Road Not Taken*, by Robert Frost.

"Matti, I came to that fork in the road of my life at age eighteen. The Holy Spirit prompted me to accept Jesus and walk on the road of His righteousness. At that same time, He placed a call on my life."

Sitting in a straight-back chair, she faced Brother Shad and smiled at this recollection of a poem learned in his Canadian school days. She could see today began as one of his good days, a day to discuss end-of-life, eternal matters. She continued a conversation from days earlier when she showed concern for Brother Shad's deceased wife Katy and her method of burial.

"When you buried Katy, did you buy two gravesites?"

"Yes. We purchased a large tombstone with both our names engraved on it. Although, my final date does not yet appear."

"What color of tombstone did you choose?"

"Rose granite with a picture of an angel engraved in both the upper right and in the upper left corners." Brother Shad used his hands to help picture his response. "A large cross engraved between our names on the front side highlights our names. The family name, Milburn, appears engraved on the backside."

"Did you and Tammy decide upon any pre-need, that is, pre-paid funeral arrangements?"

"What do you mean?" Her question surprised him.

"Pre-need arrangements mean you pick out your casket, decide a few other details, set an estimated price on some items like flowers, etc., before your funeral. With variable prices for a funeral, you can pre-pay to a point of anticipated or expected expense.

"For example, a person can confirm pre-set prices for the hearse, chapel, minister's, and musician's fees. But flowers and transportation fees to the gravesite might vary as opposed to the fixed fee charges."

"May I inquire, do you plan to bury me before I die? Or put me in a box sometime soon?" He dropped his head in order to look at her over the top of his glasses.

"No, Brother Shad. You know I love you like a sister."

"Then, why do you talk to me this way?" His agitation bordered on considering her comments an insult to his intelligence.

"Your last wishes for a funeral service and for burial will help Tammy weather the emotional storm of your loss. Consider "pre-planning" as a good business procedure. Therefore, no misunderstandings may occur among your family members."

"What do you mean -- misunderstanding?" His knuckles turned white from clinched fists. *I have never been a part of this type of conversation. Shall I terminate the discussion or allow Matti to continue?*

"Well, do you wish to be cremated or buried in a casket and vault?"

"I desire to follow 1 Corinthians 15:42–44: 'The body is sown in corruption, it is raised in incorruption. It is sown in dishonor, it is raised in glory. It is sown in weakness, it is raised in power. It is sown a natural body, it is raised a spiritual body. There is a natural body, and there is a spiritual body.' This means, as wheat grows in a field, we must place seed in the ground in order to gain a harvest. Likewise, if you bury my body in the ground, a spiritual body shall arise."

"Well spoken, Brother Shad." She spoke in a solemn manner to keep his attention. "However, many individual burial plans today designate cremation."

"I don't want cremation nor do I desire to donate any parts of my body to science or for transplant purposes."

"Please don't become angry with me, Brother Shad. I want you to know that estimates for cremation now include an average of 33 percent of all funerals nationwide. The cost totals about one-fifth to one-quarter the expense of an average casket-type burial."[1]

"Okay, now I follow your rationale." *But why did Matti bring up this entire subject? I have my burial plot. Is it not enough for my demise?* He scratched his head, unable to completely follow her logic.

"Should you change your mind, a cremation urn set in an urn vault could be placed in your grave plot by your tombstone. Or, your ashes with the owner's permission could be thrown to the wind and deposited on a farmer's field. But you may not request or allow disposal of your ashes into a lake, river, or stream.

I must keep his attention before he stops me. "I must add, I don't think Tammy would express happiness if your urn of ashes resided on a shelf in her living room."

Matti had planned this conversation with Shad for two weeks. She knew it would irritate him, but she felt impressed she must bring the matter to his attention. Even today, she prayed over every word and utterance, aware he might collapse with a stroke if angered beyond reason.

"I don't see any dignity about cremation." He placed both hands at the back of his neck and sighed, "Only a savings in burial expenses."

"Perhaps, yes. However, I would ask you again: did you and Tammy discuss your final wishes for the settlement of your estate? That includes the details of your burial."

"No." Rubbing his forehead, he thought, *I have no goods, no real estate, no instruments to divide up or even fight over.*

"Why don't you give it some thought? Pre-need plans save money in view of possible increased expenses in the future. Both of you can cooperate in the arrangements. Both of you then will know what to expect about financial and personal arrangements. You, in addition, can receive an updated will because of your pre-need plans."

"I shall consider your suggestions, Matti, since I rely on you for assistance. *Perhaps I should talk with Tammy about these end-of-life matters.* I thank you for your continued help for me every day. *I don't want to cause problems or more stress for her.* I don't always agree with you, but I appreciate your good advice." *Tammy's challenges with Melody and her library job bring enough struggles into her life.*

A BUSINESS DISCUSSION AT DOLLYS

Dark billowy clouds parted and rays of sunlight illuminated crystals on untracked snow. Three inches of snow had fallen during the night. Aunt Matti inhaled a deep breath and looked out the window beside Brother Shad, frosted with ice at its edges from the humidity in the room.

The brilliance of the day encouraged Matti, "Brother Shad, may I invite you to Dolly's Ice Cream Parlor for a chicken sandwich, coffee, and a heaped-full dish of mint chocolate-chip ice cream? If we go now, we could arrive before the early lunch crowd."

"Our conversation this morning weighed me down. Rather heavy for me, like a deep theological discussion. It did indeed create an appetite in my stomach for ice cream. I accept with pleasure."

"Make yourself presentable. I'll go drive the car up to the front door. Come, when ready and join me there. I'll wait for you under the overhang."

Later, the warmth of Dolly's Ice Cream parlor took the chill off their short walk through the snow on the parking lot. They sat at an inner booth, comfortable again, and waited for a waiter to call their number. Aunt Matti looked out the windows of the restaurant and remembered Brother Shad's recitation of the two possible paths a person's life might pursue.

She said: "I remember a poem about winter I learned in my high school days, *The Snow Storm*, by Ralph Waldo Emerson. It aptly described my growing up days walking to school on bitter cold days.

"Matti, I didn't know you enjoyed poetry. You show excellent taste. In my high school senior English class, we learned several poems. During my senior-class graduation service our pastor used the poem I quoted earlier.

"I remember his words for all of us, even to this day: 'One road leads to hell; the other road leads to eternal life.' After his message, some of the boys ran to the altar for salvation; unsaved girls cried. His message caused a revival to break out in my hometown."

Aunt Matti interrupted his observations. "Let me go pick up our order. The waitress flashed our number on the wall. Excuse me for a moment, please. I shall go pay for the food and come right back."

While he waited for Aunt Matti's return, Brother Shad turned his eyes away from the bright sunshine reflected on the icy snow and watched a young boy clear dishes from the table in the next booth. "Young man, would it be possible to close the shade on that window over there, please? The sun makes an uncomfortable reflection on my face."

"Of course, sir."

"Thank you, son."

"Brother Shad, this food looks delicious." Matti returned faster than Brother Shad expected. "Please ask the Lord to bless it. I feel hungry. My breakfast this morning consisted only of coffee and cereal."

He pronounced his usual in-depth oration which left no doubt the Lord received sufficient thanks and appreciation for his provision. But as they finished their chicken sandwiches and savored their second cup, Shad asked Aunt Matti: "What funeral arrangements did you make? Cremation or burial in the conventional manner? Did you make pre-need arrangements for yourself? What burial site did you choose?"

She did not expect him to ask these questions. But, swallowed the last mouthful of her sandwich and replied: "Dan and I purchased two lots just before his death in September 1994. Like your arrangements in Mitchell, South Dakota, we purchased a rose granite headstone similar to the one you have for Katy and yourself.

"I may have my body cremated and the urn placed in an urn vault in our burial plot beside Dan's vault. If I do that, I won't need to buy a regular size, big vault and I wouldn't have a graveside service. I must watch my money for living expenses, as do a large number of older persons. I pay out much, but little interest comes in.

"The reason I brought up this topic earlier today, next week I shall meet with my nephew to review my will. I did not update it after Dan died. Now, I plan to make pre-need arrangements with Holms, Bailey, and Turner Funeral Home. A salesman friend who works for HB & T told me he would match whatever prices Howard and Holmut Funeral Home might quote. He feels HB & T will provide more services than the H & H Funeral Home."

"Just dying can become a complicated procedure."

"Brother Shad, I hope you will talk with Tammy about pre-need funeral possibilities. It can reduce much heartache at the time of your death and make the transition for family members easier to bear at that stressful time in their lives."

"I can see I will rest better each night and know my family and I prepared well for my demise before Jesus comes and takes me home."

"Well, look at that," Aunt Matti smiled. "I can see the bottom of my ice cream dish. Did you find the bottom of yours?"

"Yes," he licked his lips, "good to the last spoonful."

Matti stood up, pulled on her coat and said, "Let's return to the Center. Your eyes tell me you need a nap."

Brother Shad entered his room and looked out his window at a bright red cardinal which sat on the stone ledge at the side of the snow-covered, frozen fish-pond. It fanned its tail, cocked its head, and checked for seeds in the nearby feeder. As he contemplated the bird's graceful movements in this wintry scene, Brother Shad's heart beat with joy.

The thought came to his mind: *In this dreary, world, God sent an elegant bird to bring life and happiness to others and myself. In a similar way, in this sin-stained world, God places His glory in the heart of everyone who accepts His Son's gift of eternal life and peace.*

The patriarch lay on his right side, faced the window, and hoped to catch another glimpse of the male cardinal before he drifted into sleep. "Well, I declare," he spoke as if Matti stood in the room. "I think he parades around that feeder in order to give pleasure to both of us. But where did his mate go? If both sat together at the feeder, the scene would make a remarkable post-card picture."

Drowsy eyelids closed. The retired preacher rolled onto his back. In moments his heavy rhythmic breathing became whistling snores. With muscles relaxed, deep sleep overcame his consciousness, a toe twitched like a dog chasing a rabbit. A Canadian farm fall scene formed in his mind—bird hunting season.

"Aaron, let's walk over by that wood pile. I believe we can scare up a couple of pheasants hidden in the grass which surrounds the area. You walk around the other side. If a rooster flies to the right, you shoot. If it flies on the left, I'll shoot."

"Okay, Shad. We each have two birds. Let's bag two more for our limits."

BANG! BANG!

"Brother Shad," Nurse Hotchkiss spoke in soft tones. "I must wake you up for your afternoon pill and snack. Sorry, you slept nice and deep."

"I dreamed my brother and I just completed our limit of pheasants up on our Canadian farm. Do you like pheasant?"

"We considered it a delicacy when I grew up," Nurse Hotchkiss remembered. "But for two winters in a row, the snow and cold killed most of the bird population around my hometown."

"That happened to us in Canada. Thereafter, we tried to provide thick habitat and food for the game birds each winter. Several farmers around us participated in that conservation practice."

"Brother Shad, you should walk around the corridors before dinner this evening. You need more indoor exercise."

"Yes, Ma'am," Brother Shad agreed. He stood up and replied, "I shall do it without hesitation."

VICTORY IN SIGHT

TUESDAY, NOVEMBER 20, 7:00 A.M.

Aunt Matti did not want to step out of her cozy bed. "Did someone need prayer? Did it cause me a restless night? Or did I eat the wrong thing yesterday for my 8 p.m. dinner?"

She knew the telephone call which awakened her had come from Brother Shad. His calls arrived between seven and seven-thirty in the mornings. Aunt Matti picked up the receiver. "What might cause a problem for you today," she said, her voice weak, her throat dry.

"Matti," Brother Shad spoke with a muffled unsteady voice. "Tall Man and Big Guy appeared beside my bed this morning. It happened as I woke up. It excited me. I thought today God designated as my day. Like before, Big Guy did not speak, he just looked at me.

"Tall man quoted Scripture to me. 'Be anxious for nothing . . . guard your heart and mind through Christ Jesus' (Philippians 4:6, 7). Then he said: 'Walk circumspectly . . . redeeming the time' (Ephesians 5:15, 16).

"As I began to contemplate what he meant, they both turned and walked out of my room. Matti, I saw a glow about them, a radiance that lit up the area which surrounded my bed."

Matti, now awake, sat up in her bed, eyes wide open, and asked: "What does the visitation signal to you, Brother Shad? What other information did they convey?"

"Tall Man, the communicative one, expressed great love through his eyes. I did not fear this encounter. I feel they set a period of time for me yet on earth before Jesus calls, because of what Tall Man said."

"Brother Shad, I suggest you pray much about the message of this visit. The Lord said something to you that requires a response. What do you think He desires on your behalf?"

"Right now, I need my breakfast and some time to consider the importance of these two Scriptures. I shall pray and ask the Holy Spirit for guidance. I know my reaction shall be of utmost consequence. Matti, my breakfast tray just arrived. I'll sign off for this time."

"I'm glad you called, Brother Shad. I'll stop by later this morning. God bless."

Matti looked at her telephone, pondered the old man's call, and thought to herself: *What happened to my dear friend earlier this morning? He expressed no problem. His excitement overflowed because of this spiritual event.*

"I better fix breakfast for myself. A cup of coffee, some fruit juice, and a hot muffin with peach jam will help me start my day. I wonder. What spiritual assignment, what spiritual victory will my aged friend achieve before he sees the glory of heaven?

"Ow! How did they make this coffee so hot today?" Brother Shad spoke out loud to himself. "I think it went through the machine twice. But it's wonderful, marvelous, and tasty." Each time he tried to take a sip, he blew little puffs of air across the top of the scalding liquid in an attempt to cool down his favorite ingredient of breakfast.

The scrambled eggs even had consistency this morning; no watery runoff around the edges. He shook his head sidewise a few times in disbelief, then ate his breakfast, and smiled: "The Lord has blessed me doubly today, a fine breakfast and an angelic visitation this morning."

The scriptural words from Tall Man came to his mind. They bombarded his thoughts with each mouthful. He thought to himself: *I believe the Holy Spirit wants me to talk to Theda this morning. I will give it one more try. She does need Jesus in her heart.*

THEDA'S CLARITY OF MIND

With breakfast finished, teeth brushed and face shaved, Brother Shad sat down in his lounge chair. He could always think well when he sat in his favorite chair. Those words from Tall Man again pounded his consciousness: *Redeem the time!*

He told himself, "I shall first read my Bible, only three chapters this morning, not 12. After I cap it with prayer, then I shall go find Theda. I know the Holy Spirit will help me. Even though she suffers from dementia, I sense the urge to share God's Word with her one more time."

In a few minutes He arose and ambled down the corridor to Theda's room, four doorways away on the right side. He announced his presence with a light tap-tap-tap on her door and said, "Good morning, Theda."

"Young man," Theda spoke with hesitation, "did you come to bring me news of my son, Sammy? I know he will come today to take me home. You know, we live in St. Paul."

"I did not see him, Theda. But I have good news about another Son who wants to take you to His home."

"You mean my son Sammy will not come for me?"

Shad sat down in a chair in front of Theda and looked at her eyes with compassion. "I mean that another Son by the name of Jesus wants to take you to His home in heaven. He wants to share it with you."

"But can't my son Sammy come and take care of me in our home in St. Paul?"

"Jesus wants you both with Him in His special home," Shad explained patiently, "a home for all of us."

"I don't know what to think about that idea. Say, young man, can a person play checkers there in that special home you call heaven?"

"One thing, Theda, I know for sure." This time he gave Theda an encouraging smile and pat on her arm. "You won't need your wheelchair. Jesus' Word has guaranteed us no more pain when we reside with Him." Brother Shad did his best to assure Theda of the importance that we all make preparations to go to this new residence, this heavenly home.

"Theda, I read about Jesus, the Son of God every day as I sit in my chair. He promises us a new life with himself, a life where we will join our family members for all eternity." Shad held his hands open and moved his fingers as if reading a book. "In fact, each of us will become a part of His great family, if each one of us will accept His leadership."

"You're confusing me, young fellow." Theda rubbed her finger up and down on the side of her nose. "If I have my own family, how can I be a part of someone else's family?"

"Theda, God made it possible for all of us to join His special family by the acceptance of the provision His Son Jesus made for us almost 2,000 years ago on the cross at Calvary."

"What provision? And why a cross at Calvary?" This statement caught her attention.

"Jesus died on a cross by crucifixion in Jerusalem at a place we call Mount Calvary."

"Why would He do that?"

"Because He loved each one of us. It became the one way He could open up heaven for you and me, and for all our family members who accept the fact that Jesus died for our sins."

"I remember something about the name Jesus," she said, rolling her eyes toward the ceiling, searching her memory for an answer. "Although, my mind seems fuzzy. However, because you tell me these facts, my knowledge of Jesus seems important."

"Jesus sent me to tell you He wants you to accept His provision for your eternal life with Him."

"I remember a Sunday school class." She pondered all he had said, scratched her head, and pursed her lips. "My teacher, Mrs. Pentzholm, told me the same story. But in a short time thereafter, my family left that town. I didn't hear the story of Jesus again until now."

"Jesus feels your decision to accept His love for you needs declaration this morning. When you believe in Him and accept His provision for the forgiveness of your sins, He takes the bad things you did in your life and washes it all away. In like manner, each one of us then become acceptable to the Father in heaven to live with His heavenly family."

"Young man, I see you read your Bible every time I pass by your open door. I receive a good sense of comfort when I pass by you in the corridor. Therefore, while I don't understand every fact you tell me, I know in my heart your intentions remain correct and honorable in what you say. I accept your proposal."

"Theda, please repeat this short prayer after me and thus make your decision official with Jesus."

"Okay."

Shad folded his hands. "Dear Jesus . . . please forgive my sins." Theda understood and repeated each phrase of the prayer. "My bad life. . . . I accept . . . what You did on the Cross . . . for me. . . . I want You . . . to be . . . my Lord and Savior. . . . Amen!" Through her dementia and increase of the Alzheimer's affliction, the Lord gave her wisdom to recognize the truth of this world event of two millennia ago.

"I want to leave a gospel tract with you, Theda. It explains what you accomplished this morning as you accepted Jesus as your Lord and Savior. Will you accept it and read it?"

"Okay."

"After you read it, please ask Chaplain Sinclair for a large print Bible. He will be happy to give you a Bible."

"I never owned a Bible."

"Please begin to read your Bible in the Book of Luke. Chaplain Sinclair can help. I suggest you read a few verses each day."

"I'll do it, young man. And don't forget to blow your nose when you leave."

Brother Shad knew the conversation complete, his dismissal final. "See you next time, Theda." He turned around, ambled back to his room, and rejoiced for another soul bound for heaven. The words of *Fairest Lord Jesus* overflowed his mind and emotional happiness at Theda's decision, *I will cherish and honor You, Jesus.*

Charles T. Clauser

THANKSGIVING DAY PLANS

Aunt Matti realized she needed more time today to drive to the Center, because the day remained foggy, the roads icy. The warmth of the car heater felt good on her legs as she drove the usual twenty minutes to the retirement complex. As she drove, her mind became absorbed with the lives of people she planned to visit.

Her thoughts today began the assimilation of details for the family Thanksgiving Day dinner scheduled for 1 p.m., two days hence. Tammy and Melody invited her to join them, along with Brother Shad, for their turkey feast. As a single lady who lived alone, and with no other celebration plans, she accepted the invitation with pleasure.

Her approach to a yellow light at a major intersection drew her attention away from the proposed dinner plans. She stopped for the red light, snapped the first three fingers together on her right hand, and spoke out loud in triumph.

"I shall go to Benson's Supermarket today and buy a pumpkin pie and a two-quart container of peach ice cream. Then I'll call Tammy this evening when she arrives home from her work to see what else I might contribute to the cause, perhaps a tossed salad or mixed vegetable from Benson's Deli."

The icy road conditions demanded her full attention. It caused her to set aside dinner preparations. Aunt Matti passed three cars which had slid off the four-lane highway, drivers still in their cars. She drove with the two right wheels, front and back, on the gravel shoulder for better traction. Her normal drive time to Brother Shad's residence became extended to one hour.

Exhausted when she arrived at the Center parking lot, she stepped with care out of her car. Ted, the buildings and ground assistant supervisor, walked nearby. He had sprinkled salt on the walkways and at the edges of nearby cars. He took her arm and escorted her to the front door of the Center.

"Whew. Thank you, Ted."

"You're welcome, Matti. Please be most careful as you walk about today."

"My drive out this morning—horrible," she replied, "beyond adequate description."

NEW LIFE

Brother Shad entered the door of his room, his reflection continued: *Many people live here, Lord. They need You. I pray more persons will accept Your free gift of salvation. Holy Spirit, move on others as you did in Theda's life this morning.*

The old pastor looked at his watch—10:20 a.m. Time for Matti to stop by. He stared out his window for a few minutes, noticed the frost around the edge of the pane, and muttered: "It looks like the snow came down heavy last night. With frost on the window, ice may cover the highways. Lord, protect Matti."

As the elder statesman turned to sit down in his shabby, worn lounge chair, he heard the familiar click-clomp of shoes increase in volume in the corridor. Aunt Matti marched right into his room and, without invitation, promptly sat down in his guest chair. Their eyes met and expressed mutual admiration. Aunt Matti spoke first: "Brother

Shad, did any extraordinary event happened since you called me earlier this morning?"

"Yes, Matti. The Holy Spirit prompted me to speak to Theda, fourth room down on the right, just a few minutes before you arrived."

"Oh, I thought she couldn't think or speak well."

"She accepted Jesus this morning. The Holy Spirit opened her thought processes to grasp the truth of the gospel. She no longer lives in the kingdom of darkness."

"Marvelous," she exclaimed. "Did the Holy Spirit prompt you to talk with someone else?"

"He impressed me to pray for someone. I do not know who. But I feel my prayers will help to prepare that person, whomever, for making a salvation decision."

"Our wonderful Lord continues to use us in His mighty army, in spite of our ages, to ensure the family of God grows and grows." She clapped her hands together a couple of times, and raised them in the air as a sign of praise to the Lord.

"Yes, Matti. Oh Matti, look, in the doorway! Tall Man and Big Guy came in again."

Brother Shad raised an arm in greeting, beckoned them with his hand, and said: "Come in, gentlemen! Please meet my dear friend, Matti."

Matti's eyes opened wide in astonishment as she looked toward the doorway and reacted in bewilderment. "Brother Shad, I see no one."

"Matti, Tall Man said they came to take me to Jesus. We leave now. Good-bye, Mat—!" With that announcement, his head slumped forward, his hands dropped lifeless onto his lap across his Bible.

"Brother Shad. What happened? Do you feel sick?" She stood up, alarmed at what had just transpired. "I shall call the nurse. Don't worry. Nurse Hotchkiss and Dr. Murray will take good care of you." The event occurred before Matti could decide how to respond. She thought she heard Brother Shad say "good-bye." Perhaps he did give her an indication of what happened.

Nurse Hotchkiss arrived within seconds. She tried to take Brother Shad's pulse—no response at his wrist . . . nothing at his neck . . . no movement at his ankle. She unbuttoned his shirt. With stethoscope to his chest and back—no sounds.

"Matti," Nurse Hotchkiss spoke in undertones, a tear blurred her eyesight. "Our patriarch in Room 15 left for his Maker. Brother Shad's heart in straight-forward words, stopped its rhythmic beat."

Matti bent over her friend and with care lifted the open Bible from under the aged minister's fingers and off his lap. Tears trickled down her cheeks. Torrents soon ran down her face and moistened the verses of his open Bible: *The LORD is my shepherd. . . . Yea, though I walk through the valley of the shadow of death, I will fear no evil; for you are with me* (Psalm 23:1, 4).

Matti kneeled down beside his chair. She grasped his hand, and with her head on his arm, realized, *I'm alone again.*

"Good-bye, dear friend. Until Jesus comes for me, and we meet again with Katy and Dan, I shall miss you every day.

"Please remember, Prince, I love you."

THE END

EPILOGUE – FIVE YEARS LATER

Stalwart Aunt Matti continues her regular care-giving visits at the City Center Retirement Home. Friends desire her words of encouragement, meaningful prayers, and knowledgeable insights into dietary health practices.

Daughter Tammy rejected two recent marriage proposals, but remained committed to her directorship at the Shiplane and Beavershead Community Library.

Granddaughter Melody graduated with a master's degree in business administration and seeks further education at a not too distant law school, Baylor University.

Henry and Phillip, Brother Shad's dinner partners, both died of loneliness this last year.

Sandra Ridenhorst grieves yet for Sid, her departed husband. No resolution appears in sight. She lost thirty pounds, does not care for any kind of food, and eats just a minimum amount to stay alive.

Mrs. Penderholt, receptionist at the City Center, enjoys conversations with "her birdies," says it keeps her in good humor.

Nurse Hotchkiss retired this year and commented: "Brother Shad gave her excellent spiritual insights." He remains her favorite and most memorable resident.

Chris Carpenter, a frequent visitor, received one of Brother Shad's Bibles. The River Front church congregation at First and Elm elected him as their leader four years ago.

Pete, Brother Shad's Thursday morning brunch partner, received election two years ago as secretary for the governing body of their world-wide fellowship.

END NOTES

PREFACE

1. *A Profile of Older Americans: 2012*, Administration on Aging, Department of Health and Human Services. Modified: April 17, 2013. Principal sources of data for the Profile are the U.S. Census Bureau, the National Center for Health Statistics, and the Bureau of Labor Statistics. The Profile incorporates recent data available, but not all items are updated on an annual basis. http://www.AoA.gov/AofARoot/Aging_Statistics/Profile/2012/2.aspx Statistics identify a new culture of aging in the United States:

"*The older population (65+) numbered 41.4 million in 2011, [is] an increase of 6.3 million or 18% since 2000.

*The number of Americans aged 45-64 – who will reach 65 over the next two decades – [will] increase by 33% during this period.

*Over one in every eight [persons], or 13.3%, of the population is an older American.

*The population 65 and over has increased from 35 million in 2000 to 41.4 million in 2011 (an 18% increase) and is projected to increase to 79.7 million in 2040.

*The 85+ population is projected to increase from 5.7 million in 2011 to 14.1 million in 2040."

CHAPTER 12—"Salvation Settles Destiny"

1. Information concerning pre-need funeral arrangements for cremations and casket-type burial was confirmed with Lenny Cope, manager with Klingner-Cope Funeral Home, 1635 N. Benton Avenue, Springfield, MO 65803. Conversation dated April 2, 2008.

AUTHOR'S BIOGRAPHY

REVEREND CHARLES T. CLAUSER ministered as an Assembly of God missionary, teacher and administrator for over 25 years in the Philippines. Earlier, he served stateside for 20 years as a music teacher and college administrator.

In 1974, Dr. Clauser joined the faculty of Trinity Bible Institute (now College), Ellendale, North Dakota and became chairman of the music department in 1976. Two years later, he began serving as acting academic dean.

Arriving in the Philippines in 1982, Charles taught at the Far East Advanced School of Theology (now Asia Pacific Theological Seminary) and at Bethel Bible College located on the same campus in Metro Manila.

Charles and Mary Clauser trained Christian workers and lay people, conducted short-term seminars for pastors, and ministered at district meetings. They also taught two- and three-week block sessions as adjunct faculty at various Bible schools in the Philippines.

Dr. Clauser taught in the Chinese Servant Leadership Institute at United Bethel Church in Manila. He served 17 years on the board of the Bible Institute for the Deaf in Metro Manila.

During their last term in the Philippines, Rev. Clauser assisted as OIC at the King's Garden Children Home located in Upper Sabatan, Orion, Bataan, Philippines. This ministry included upgrading facilities and coordinating two construction projects at the Home.

Dr. Clauser self-published a book of memoirs entitled *Family and Friends, Together Forever* (2011). Two additional books are in the process of completion. He has been a member of the Ozarks Chapter of the American Christian Writers for six years and served as its writing contest chairperson for five of those years.

The Clausers retired to Maranatha Village in Springfield, Missouri in May 2004. Their present ministry includes writing, music, and visitation at Maranatha Village and in area hospitals.

www.ingramcontent.com/pod-product-compliance
Lightning Source LLC
Chambersburg PA
CBHW051751040426
42446CB00007B/314